Dr U W (Uli) Arndt, FRS, was a research physicist, formerly a staff member of and latterly visitor in the MRC Laboratory of Molecular Biology in Cambridge, where he specialised in the design of X-ray diffraction apparatus used in the determination of the structures of biological materials. He was born in Berlin, his parents being of mixed German, Russian, Dutch and English stock. He was educated in Germany until 1936 when at the age of twelve he emigrated with his parents to England and continued his education at Dulwich College, King Edward's School, Birmingham, and Emmanuel College, Cambridge. He obtained a first degree in Physics and a doctorate in Crystallography. He then worked at Birmingham University and for thirteen years at the Royal Institution in London, moving back to Cambridge in 1963, where he worked ever since, except for sabbatical absences in the USA and in France. He and his wife, whom he met on a skiing holiday, were very happily married for forty-seven years and had three daughters and seven grandchildren. He travelled widely on business and for pleasure all over the world. His hobbies were skiing, sailing, hill-walking, sketching and reading. This is his first non-scientific publication.

PERSONAL X-RAY
REFLECTIONS

PERSONAL X-RAY REFLECTIONS

Uli Arndt

ATHENA PRESS
LONDON

ISBN 1 84401 694 3

First Published 2006 by
ATHENA PRESS
Queen's House, 2 Holly Road
Twickenham TW1 4EG
United Kingdom

Printed for Athena Press

Contents

Introduction

The Chinese wish each other 'may you not live in interesting times'. I have lived through interesting and dangerous times, but I have mostly had the good fortune of having been in the right place at the right time and have remained, relatively, unscathed. Not only have both I and my immediate family escaped having awful things done to us, but I have also escaped being forced into the abhorrent actions or into the criminal behaviour which have made it so difficult for many of my contemporaries to live with their consciences.

I was born in Germany just after the horrendous inflation of the 1920s but I never went hungry then or during the subsequent depression. My own lot was improved, rather than adversely affected, when my parents emigrated, with me, from Nazi Germany to England where I received what is now called a 'privileged education' at a time when that helped, rather than blighted, one's career. I was not interned during World War II as an enemy alien, nor did I have to fight. I had the great luck of being able to pursue a career which I loved and all my life have been paid for doing work which was also my hobby and which introduced me to many interesting people and places.

My greatest good fortune was a marvellous marriage to Valerie who was a wonderful wife and who gave birth to three lovely daughters who in turn presented us with seven much-loved, loving and talented grandchildren.

Until the last few years we enjoyed reasonably good health and while we were never rich we were never prevented by financial considerations from living the sort of life we wanted to live. The good fortune lasted until my eightieth year. For forty seven years I never came home without having something to tell Valerie or something I wanted to consult or argue with her about. Now that I no longer have her, I am writing this as a very poor substitute for talking things over with her.

I am glad that I was able to exercise my profession as a research scientist in research institutes rather than in university departments so that I could devote nearly all my time to my own work rather than to administrative and teaching duties. Much of my working life has been concerned with the determination of the structure of molecules by observing and measuring the reflection of X-rays by crystals – hence my title.

To be strictly honest, I have done rather little of the observing and measuring of X-ray reflections myself. Rather, I have designed and built instruments and devised new methods to make it easier for my colleagues to carry out these observations and measurements. This field of instrument design for X-ray crystallography has been sufficiently competitive to be interesting but not so much so that there was constant cutthroat rivalry. I have been successful enough in my work to be moving in circles where I have met and known many of the great and famous in science. Being of a lower status myself, I have had time to sit back and look around, to enjoy family life and the acquaintance and the diverse views of interesting people from many countries.

I benefited by having been a pupil of Sir Lawrence Bragg who more or less started off the subject of X-ray crystallography and I have worked for many years in the laboratory founded by Max Perutz, who won a joint Nobel Prize with John Kendrew for the first structure determinations of proteins. My own work has helped to make subsequent structure determinations easier.

Scientists are not generally conformists. I well remember a conference where I was only interested in part of the programme, and where I spent a lot of time in the anteroom of the lecture theatre talking about politics and international affairs to other delegates. I never talked to a single Russian who had ever been a communist, a single Briton who supported Margaret Thatcher, any American who owned up to having voted Republican or any German opposed to German reunification. Perhaps this non-conformism is the explanation of the limited impact which scientists have on government policy.

I believe that most scientists can be classified as being either 'knowers' or 'doers". The 'knowers' are interested in the whole of their subject; they read widely around the field and they are diligent attenders at all colloquia and seminars. They finish up with a wide knowledge of their field and, because of this width, they may not be amongst the most original of thinkers though they may be excellent teachers. The 'doers' interest is in what they are doing themselves: their thinking and their reading centres on what is needed for their immediate research projects in the way of experimental and mathematical techniques; their knowledge may be quite narrow. They get their enjoyment from what they are doing at the time in the same way as a child playing with a construction set. They do not necessarily care whether someone else has trodden the path before them, so long as they have the pleasure of solving their own problem by themselves. I place myself quite emphatically among the 'doers'.

The really great scientists alternate between knowing and doing phases. It always seemed to me that my long-term colleague and boss, Max Perutz, was a single-minded and narrow 'doer' who concentrated only on the structure of haemoglobin until it was solved. After that he read and thought much more widely in the whole field of molecular biology and outside it.

JD Bernal explained the difference between the two classes quite clearly on an occasion when I was sitting with a group of his Birkbeck College students after a conference session in which he had made his usual brilliant contribution to the discussion. One of his people – to whom he was always just 'Sage' – said to him, 'Sage, you are the most intelligent man I have ever met and you have made great contributions to science, but not quite as great as one might have expected from you; why is that?' After thinking for a moment he answered, 'I have always had a passionate interest in everything that goes on in science and I have found that in a given amount of time I can read very much more about what others have done than I can hope to do by myself.'

After Royal Institution Friday evening discourses we often amused ourselves by classifying the lecturers into one of two groups, similar to, but by no means congruent with, my classes of 'knowers' and 'doers'. Some of the speakers were obviously grateful for their good fortune, which had enabled them to have worked on the interesting subject which they were describing. Others clearly felt that it was lucky for their field of study that they had devoted their abilities to it.

In the following pages I have tried to relate how my life and thoughts have been shaped by my experiences inside and outside my career as a research scientist during my first eight decades.

I should like to express my thanks to my three daughters, Elizabeth, Caroline and Annabel, who have encouraged me to get down to writing. They, and my colleagues Wanda Bullock, Andrew McLachlan, Martin Kyte and Ian Walker, have made many helpful suggestions and criticisms of my manuscript. I am grateful to Joyce Fordham, for allowing me to quote her appreciation of Max and Gisela Perutz, and to those who have given me permission to use their photographs.

My special thanks are due to Annabel Culver, Roger Lilley and to my grandchildren, Helen and Edward Lilley and Jonathan Welch, who have tried to cure my abysmal ignorance of modern computer word-processing and have helped me to operate the word-recognition program *Dragon Naturally Speaking*, which has enabled me to dictate some of my manuscript into the computer. It is always tempting for the old to think that the young these days are born with an expertise in subjects such as computing or word processing. When that thought occurs to me I try to remember a laboratory seminar, sixty years ago, when Professor Dame Kathleen Lonsdale described some lengthy experiments which she had carried out on a visit to the USA in order to determine the counting losses of a Geiger counter at high counting rates. I could see from her results that these losses were due to a time constant of about a hundred microseconds in the electronic circuitry which she had used. When I pointed this out, I hope very politely, my supervisor, Will Taylor, said to her, 'Well, the young these days are born with a knowledge of electronics.' I take great credit for not telling him then that I had spent much time in gaining a body of knowledge, which some of my elders had perhaps been too lazy to acquire.

Early years in Germany, 1924–1936

My full name is Ulrich Wolfgang Arndt. Outside Germany, there are not many people who can pronounce, let alone spell, these names. I have always called myself Uli, the normal abbreviation of Ulrich. I myself make this rhyme with woolly. Others make it rhyme with July or coolie. I am also accustomed to being addressed as Olly by those who think that my name is an abbreviation of Oliver. A polite Spaniard who considers it disrespectful to shorten names always calls me Ulysses. So I answer to 'Hi' or, in fact, any loud cry.

I was born in Berlin in 1924 into what now seems a remote era – two years before Lindbergh made the first solo crossing of the Atlantic and two years also before the first regular sound broadcasting service from the London transmitter 2LO. It was a time when very few ordinary city dwellers owned a motorcar and when, judging from photographs, city streets were mostly empty of cars, moving or parked. A time when coal and milk and ice were delivered in horse-drawn carts, and would continue to be for another twenty-five years. Houses in the centre of capital cities were still partly lit by gas; my grandmother's flat in a middle-class district of Berlin would not get electric light in the kitchen for another three years.

My father, Ernst Julius Arndt, was of mixed German and Russian parentage and was born in 1887 in Zarske Selo, near St. Petersburg, where his father owned a paper mill. We always celebrated his birthday on the 8th January. On his birth certificate, which I discovered among his papers after his death, his birthday was given as the 25th December 1886. This was old style; Russia only changed to the Gregorian calendar after the Revolution. The paper mill failed in 1890 and the family moved to Berlin, where my grandfather died a few years later. The family, consisting of my grandmother, my father, and his brother, who died in his late teens, assumed, or resumed, German nationality. They were in reduced circumstances and my father had to leave school at the age of fifteen after passing his *Matura*, two years short of the *Abitur*, in order to become a commercial apprentice in a company making railway equipment. In 1908, he was sent to the United States by his firm, where he spent two happy years in Pittsburgh. There, his favourite enjoyment was horse riding, getting his mounts from a local livery stable. This stood him in good stead when he had to return to Germany to look after his mother on the death of his brother. While there, he had to do his military service, which he did in a Prussian cavalry regiment. He was called up in July 1914, serving first on the Eastern Front and later in France, finishing the war in November 1918 as a first lieutenant in the Signal Corps, having only once been lightly wounded and having been decorated with the Iron Cross, first and second class. He maintained that he had been convinced from the outset that the war was a disaster for Germany and was bound to end in a defeat. His outlook was always that of a citizen of Europe, rather than that of a narrowly nationalistic German.

After the war, he found employment in a Dutch-German company selling railway equipment and rose rapidly through middle management. Having his salary paid in Dutch guilders he was comparatively well-off during the raging German inflation. In 1921, he met and married my mother, Clara Margarethe Juliusberg, who came from a Hamburg family of mainly Dutch and German stock, and who was very remotely related to him. Owing to the post-war housing shortage, my parents started their married life in a converted fifth-floor attic flat which was cold in winter and hot in summer. I was born on the kitchen table, since hospital maternity beds were in short supply.

My mother, who was born in 1895, was a rebel and took the unusual step, much opposed by her family, of training, first as a nursery teacher and later as a hospital administrator. She had what her parents regarded as dangerously left wing views and was active in the German Socialist Party.

During the inflation, my mother's savings depreciated so much that the money with which she had intended to buy her first home barely sufficed for a set of dinner plates. The rate of inflation was so high that many people were paid every day at midday, bringing baskets to the bank to convey their piles of banknotes to the shops before the value of their earnings had evaporated.

Not very long after I was born, my father's employers' firm collapsed and he kept us going by getting some part-time jobs and half-paid positions. He wanted to emigrate to the US where he had been happy before the Great War, but the Americans operated a quota system for visas based on the applicant's country of birth. My father, having been born in St Petersburg, could not get a visa because, so soon after the Russian Revolution, the Russian quota was full. Thirty years later, I wanted to take a post-doctoral position in America and had to apply for a short period exchange visitor's visa because the German quota for a normal visa was full. By 1990 when my daughter Caroline had to move to Florida with her husband Dick the quota system had been abandoned or she might have met with restrictions under the British quota.

One of my own earliest memories is of a train journey from Berlin to Hamburg with my mother. We were travelling in a wooden-seated, third-class carriage and my ceaseless activity and noise so irritated our fellow travellers that they induced the guard to transfer us to an empty first-class compartment. I think that I can still see in my mind's eye the enormous brass key with which that dignified official unlocked the door of the compartment to thrust us into a world of luxury and red plush. There were loose cylindrical bolsters, which to me were like the barrels in which the beer was delivered to the restaurant opposite our block of flats and I whiled away the journey time playing at being a beer delivery man.

We later made the train journey to Hamburg several times to visit my mother's parents. My chief joy was being taken into the restaurant car, where each table had heavy fold-down brass rings into which one put one's glasses to stop them from falling over during a bumpy part of the ride. Half a century later, when I flew from London to Moscow, the fittings and glass shades of the Aeroflot plane reminded me vividly of the 'Mitropa' dining cars of my youth. Another early memory is of the double-decker London buses, of which a few had been delivered to Berlin as an experiment in the 1920s. I can still remember the tension when the

Berliners watched the *Englische Busse*, expecting them to overturn at the next corner. I do not remember very much else of my early days in Berlin, but, on a visit there in the 1970s, I walked past the Ufa-Palast cinema on the Kurfürstendamm and suddenly I remembered being pushed past that same cinema in my pram and seeing a display in coloured lights representing a moon rocket advertising a science fiction film.

When I was a little older, my parents often told me something of the story of a film when they had been to the cinema the evening before. I well remember their excitement when they told me that they had seen not merely moving pictures but pictures that talked and sang at the same time. The film had been Al Jolson's *The Jazz Singer*, the first 'talkie' ever made. I can also remember a visit to the zoo where a baby elephant had just been born. A fat man standing next to us in front of the cage said to me: 'That must have been a big stork that brought that elephant, little boy!'

I thought for a bit and then said, to the great amusement of the fat man, 'I don't think that the elephant was brought by a stork and I don't think that storks are really strong enough to bring any babies.'

In due course I went to a kindergarten in Berlin-Dahlem; it was one run according to the Montessori method, in which carefully designed learning toys were put out in the room and we were encouraged to pick up whatever we fancied. Playing with boxes with compartments containing sticks in ascending order taught us our numbers and the elements of arithmetic. Then there were cards on which letters cut out from sandpaper had been stuck and we learnt their shapes by tracing them with our eyes shut.

By the time I was six, and had made the transition from Montessori kindergarten to Montessori school, I could read and write reasonably well. This was unusual in Germany, where reading and writing in most schools only started at the age of six. The main sign that I was at a proper school was that on the first day I was presented with the traditional *Schultüte*, a large conical bag filled with chocolates and sweets, marking the beginning of the serious part of schooling for all children. I had only had two terms at the Montessori school when my father, at last, landed a management job with Carl Schenck, manufacturers, then and now, of weighing, testing and balancing machines. The company was based in Darmstadt, the capital of the *Land* of Hessen, and we moved there. The Hessian dialect was so different from the 'high' German that I was accustomed to that my father's new colleagues all advised him that I would not understand a word and would not be understood if I went to a public elementary school in Darmstadt and I must go to a more refined private school.

Unfortunately, the director of the recommended school turned out to be not only old-fashioned, but also violently xenophobic, disapproving of the non-German methods of the Italianate Montessori school. I had been taught to write and read the international cursive script, whereas my new school used the angular old German script in which, for example, the word *immer* (always) is written with eleven successive up-and-down hooks. What was worse, instead of writing in notebooks, we had to write with a stylus on a slate engraved with parallel guidelines. Stylus and crayons had to lie on the desk with the points to the right and both feet under the desk had to be parallel. Any infringements were punished with a sharp slap.

After the free and easy discipline of the Montessori school, I did not take very much to my dragon of a teacher. The feeling was clearly reciprocated and it was only a matter of time before the explosion came. The teacher's favourite butt was a mousy girl with a bad squint. The teacher knew she could always draw sycophantic laughter from the class by an unpleasant joke at the expense of 'cross-eyed Matilda'. After one such incident I said in a loud voice that it was silly and cruel to ridicule someone for their appearance, which they could not help. I was told that my behaviour was quite unacceptable and that, at the end of term, everyone would get a 'one' for behaviour (meaning very good) except for Hans, the lout of the class, who would get a 'two' (good on the whole), and Uli, who would get a 'three' (barely satisfactory).

I shouted back, 'While you are about it, why not a five?' (inadequate). At that, I was hit over the head with a book and locked up in a dark closet, while my enemy shouted outside, 'You can tell your father that you cannot come back on Monday.'

My parents had, in the meantime, made their own arrangements and on Monday I started at another school which had only six pupils but which was owned and run by a kindly old lady who was a born teacher, under whom I spent two and a half happy years. There were snags, of course: the new school used the cursive alphabet and I had to make a switch back to what I had been taught to forget.

My other problem was music. I have never been able to hold a tune and was much too clumsy to play an instrument. At school concerts, I was always instructed just to mouth the words of the songs but never to make a sound. At subsequent schools I encountered optimistic music teachers who tried out the new boy by making me sing scales. After my first attempt, I was always told pretty firmly: 'No, you will do drawing instead of music' and that suited me very well.

During my last year at primary school, my mother asked the teacher what she thought would become of me. She got the answer, 'You need not ask; of course Uli will become an *Akademiker.*' That is, go into a job that requires a university training.

The early 1930s were a period of political unrest. The older part of the town, the *Altstadt*, was reputedly entirely inhabited by communists. It was regarded as a no-go area for anyone dressed in bourgeois clothes. Unemployment was very high and the unemployed stretched out their benefit payment by doing menial jobs. During the cold winters, it was the German custom to flood tennis courts to turn them into ice rinks. There was always a crowd of unemployed men who, for a few pfennigs, would clamp ice skates to the boots of middle-class children. I gather that the winters are no longer cold enough for this cheap and convenient method of making ice rinks. The summers were more than likely to be enlivened by shoot-outs between uniformed gangs of Nazi Brownshirts and Communists or Socialists. My mother and I were once obliged to shelter behind a monument in the centre of Darmstadt while the bullets were flying.

Soon after we moved to Darmstadt in 1930, our stalwart north German maid, Martha, who had come with us to settle us in, had to return to her home and my mother had to interview a local girl.

Martha strongly advised against a girl whom she had spotted on the way to our house, escorted by a Brownshirt. My mother took the risk and the Brownshirt turned out to be one of the many unemployed who had been lured into the Nazi party by the promise of being found a job by the party: he became a firm friend for whom my father later found a job at Schenck's when he married Anny, the maid.

I have few memories of any of the houses in which I lived as a child, largely because I spent so little time indoors. My mother was an open air fanatic. She firmly believed that, to keep healthy, all children should spend at least five hours a day outdoors. My homework was always done on the balcony – in winter I would wear an overcoat and gloves and be wrapped up in an additional blanket. My stamp collection presented some problems, as each individual pile of stamps had to be weighed down to prevent too many losses to the wind. My mother followed her own tenets: I can still see her sitting on the veranda reading aloud to me with one hand lifted up high, waiting for the doctor to come to stitch up her hand after she had cut it badly carving a leg of lamb.

My entry into the *Gymnasium* coincided with the start of the Nazi regime, and this soon made itself felt. Every lesson started with the class rising to its feet and giving the Nazi salute, which the teacher acknowledged by saying, 'Heil Hitler; you may sit down.' Nazi ideology soon found its way into the curriculum; on Saturday, normal lessons were replaced by National Socialist instruction, that is, the history of the Nazi party, the stab-in-the-back theory of the collapse of the German armies in 1918, Nazi racial theories on the superiority of Aryan peoples, and so on. I remember particularly the lessons of religious education which started with the singing of a hymn. While we stood with our hands on the desks, the teacher walked up and down, handing out indiscriminate blows from his cane onto our fingers, 'because a little Christian chastisement is good for a boy'. The lesson thereafter consisted of a novel theology in which President Hindenburg was the equivalent of God the Father, Adolf Hitler of Jesus Christ, and the German spirit now represented the Holy Ghost.

Corporal punishment was frequent, a favourite ploy of one of the most sadistic teachers being a slap on the side of the face so

19

that all five finger marks were visible to make sure that the teacher of the next class knew whom to pick on.

Schoolwork was sometimes used as a method of detecting any anti-Nazi attitudes in parents. We were once set an essay on 'What my parents talk about after I have gone to bed'. This was represented as a useful practice in stealing downstairs and listening without being detected, in case we had to act as spies for the Fatherland in the next war. Needless to say, my essay was the result of a collaboration between my parents and myself. With the ever-present danger of betrayal and denunciation, many people developed what was called *Der Deutsche Blick* (the German look), which was a rapid glance over one's shoulder to make sure that one was not overheard.

Constant surveillance was, of course, one of the features of life under a dictatorship. The Nazis instituted a series of elections, or rather plebiscites, in which the voters were asked to vote *'Ja'* or *'Nein'* to the question of whether they approved Hitler's latest action or policy. The 'yes' vote was always around ninety-five percent. I once accompanied my mother to the polling station, where the voting took place at tables in full view of the supervising staff. A large banner proclaimed: 'The German voter is not ashamed to record his vote for the Führer in public. If, however, you prefer to vote in secret you may use the cubicle in the corner of the room.' Sitting next to the cubicle was a Brownshirt with a clipboard, on which he recorded the names of the secret voters.

Everyone had heard of people who had got away scot-free in spite of having made remarks critical of the party or its leaders. But mostly one was careful not to fall foul of any regulations, by action or inaction. There was always the danger of being denounced. Thus, when my father heard of an acquaintance who had been arrested for possessing a revolver and he remembered that his own officer's revolver was in his bedside table and the amnesty period was up, my mother and I set off with the revolver at the bottom of my enamel beach bucket, well covered with sand from the sandpit, and buried it deep in the forest, far from any possible observation

My father used to say that what made the repression worse was that it was neither constant nor predictable. I was once in a tram in Darmstadt. Two Nazi stormtroopers were sitting in a corner. A somewhat inebriated old man got on and saluted the passengers with a '*Heil, Moscow*,' and the communist clenched fist salute. He then proceeded to tell a number of scurrilous anti-Nazi jokes. Everyone, Brownshirts included, roared with laughter and he got off, after two stops, quite unmolested with a final '*Heil, Moscow*'. Yet many were sent to concentration camps, such as Dachau, for far less (but not to extermination camps which were not built until later). I can recall a commonly-quoted parody of the old children's prayer

> *Lieber Gott mach mich fromm*
> *Dass ich in den Himmel komm*
> (Dear Lord, make me good / so that I get to Heaven)

which became,

> *Lieber Gott mach mich stumm*
> *Dass ich nicht nach Dachau komm*
> (Dear Lord, make me dumb / so that I don't go to Dachau)

In the 1960s, a group of European molecular biologists, including several Jews, were shown various possible German sites for the proposed European Molecular Biology Laboratory. They had no hesitation in turning down one site that was only a few miles from a signpost to Dachau.

I have often wondered how I would have withstood the enormous pressure of constant Nazi indoctrinations and propaganda if I had not had the good fortune of having a father and mother whose opposition to Hitler and his doctrines was instinctive and immediate and who, through family links and friendships in other European countries, were immune to the narrow German jingoism. Many families I knew were not equipped psychologically to resist the Nazi teaching. An example was a family of staunchly Christian *Bibelforscher* (Jehovah's witnesses), consisting of a German father and a French mother and a son and daughter, a few years older than I. The boy survived the war and, in 1945, wrote to me, full of indignation at the Allies anti-German prejudices, which made them exclude Germany from the first post-war Olympic Games. Like many young Germans, he had no idea of how the rest of the world regarded the feelings that Nazi Germany had aroused.

My parents took me on walks every Sunday in the Odenwald, the wooded hills to the east of the Rhine plain, which stretched from Darmstadt to Heidelberg. On these walks they de-indoctrinated me and introduced me to democratic ideas. Fortunately, I was sufficiently intelligent not to give my parents away during the week. Involuntary or deliberate denunciation of parents by their own children was not uncommon.

Particularly tragic were the many German Jews who were strongly patriotic Germans, and more or less completely assimilated, and to whom the idea of becoming second-class citizens was deeply wounding. They could not grasp that they had no future in Germany.

Amongst my parents' Jewish friends in Darmstadt was the family of Ernst Trier, the owner and chief designer of a long-established family business of furniture manufacturers. They had the sagacity to send their son, Peter, who was about five years older than I, to school in England in 1934, to be followed by their daughter Hannah in 1936, the same time as we came to England. Peter and Hannah spent many of their school holidays with us. I owe my first introduction to science and mathematics to Peter, who later had a most distinguished career in engineering, at first in government service and later in the Philips organisation.

The Trier parents visited us in London over Christmas 1937 and my parents tried hard to persuade them not to return to Germany, where their lives would be in danger. Ernst Trier refused on the grounds that he could not desert his workforce and his factory. Six months later he was arrested on a trumped-up charge and murdered while in prison.

My mother saw the menace of Nazism most clearly and was adamant that she did not want to go on living in Germany, nor bring up her son there. She realised early that the danger from Hitler's Nazi Party was not going to disappear quickly and she urged my father to start thinking about emigrating. It was very hard for my father to make the decision to leave Germany. He was prospering financially after having brought his company, Carl

Schenck GmbH, back from near bankruptcy. He was not yet under direct political or racial pressure, but neither of my parents could produce an *Ahnenpass*, a certificate of pure Aryan descent, since the necessary information about my parents' ancestry was in Russian and Dutch records, respectively. On the other hand, though my parents suspected that there was Jewish blood on both sides of the family, those records were not accessible to Nazi investigation either. In the meantime, I derived some benefit from the fact that my cranial measurements, as determined by my form master with a large pair of calipers, were Aryan, rather than non-Aryan. No one ever knew exactly what the word 'Aryan' meant; it was usually taken to signify 'without taint of Jewish blood'. (During the war, the Japanese were regarded as honorary Aryans.)

In the end, my father was persuaded by my mother and by events around us to emigrate. He succeeded in appointing himself British agent for the specialist machines manufactured by his company. In 1939, he negotiated the sale of the manufacturing rights to the Birmingham firm W & T Avery and became their employee, responsible for the novel dynamic balancing machines that quickly became important in the aviation industry. The status change from managing director must have been difficult for him, but his emigration 'in the interests of the German export drive' allowed us to take our possessions with us and this work of 'national importance to Britain' later preserved him from wartime internment.

In the early days of the Hitler regime, my mother's quick thinking defused a potentially dangerous situation. We were sitting on the balcony of our flat where she was helping me with my Latin homework, when a lorry with a patrol of Brownshirts came along the road below. They were carrying out a spot-check of forbidden books, which would be destroyed at one of the periodic book-burning events. Seeing us at my books, one of the troopers shouted up jocularly: 'Have you any dangerous books up there?'

'Only a Latin primer, which is only dangerous to school children,' my mother called back, and the lorry drove on to shouts of laughter, without a search of our bookshelves.

The Latin book must have been a good one. When I began school in England, three years after starting Latin in Germany, I was considerably ahead of my English contemporaries. After quite a short time I also had little more difficulty with writing essays in English than I had had in German, and my French was quite fluent as well: modern languages were only started in the *Gymnasium* after a pretty complete initiation into Latin, and I had been given French and English lessons by private tutors. I was given the opportunity of practising my languages during 'English-only' and 'French-only' walks with my parents.

History, of course, required extensive re-learning, since everything had been taught from the nationalist German point of view. I caused considerable amusement when to my English form master's question: 'Who was Marshal Blücher?' I answered 'The Prussian General who won the battle of Waterloo'! It was difficult to escape this German nationalism in my private reading. In Germany there were many more boys' books on the Nordic than on the Classical myths and in all the books about the wars, from Caesar's campaigns until World War I, Teutons and Germans were always the heroes, glorious, if victorious, and tragic, if defeated.

Valerie used to tease me that, for her, Caesar and his legions were 'we' and their German and Celtic adversaries were 'they' but, for me, as a result of my early indoctrination, it was the other way round.

My least favourite subject at school was mathematics which, up to the age of twelve, consisted only of long multiplication and division and of drill in multiplication tables. We were expected to know our tables up to nine times nineteen. I hated the hours spent on the exercises in arithmetic and I remember my delight on discovering algebra and Euclidian geometry when I came to England.

There was very little sport in Germany other than physical exercises in unison. Occasionally, we were marched off to a football ground by two teachers, who usually failed to prevent a game from developing into a free fight. I was utterly astonished on my first games afternoon in England: 600 boys were playing twenty games of rugby and there was not a teacher in sight to keep things under control.

The German slang term for a teacher was *Pauker* which means 'drummer' because he drummed knowledge into his pupils. The amount of beatings, and other forms of corporal punishment, were something that was accepted as normal, as was the overt sadism of some teachers. No one then had the extraordinary idea that school could be pleasant, let alone that schooldays were the happiest days of one's life. In compensation, there was a sort of jailbird camaraderie directed against the teachers who were seen as the enemy. Cribbing was accordingly regarded as morally correct. As I was good at most subjects, my notebooks were much in demand and I was fairly popular and had a relatively easy time.

I knew, of course, that my parents were making preparations for settling abroad, and that my additional language lessons were part of those preparations. By 1936, one was aware that there was a very real possibility of war, sooner or later. Posters about air-raid precautions and march-pasts of paramilitary Nazi organisations were common events.

One of my last memories in Darmstadt was the remilitarisation of the Rhineland. Under the Treaty of Versailles, a zone of Germany reaching beyond Darmstadt in the east was demilitarised and barred to army units. In March 1936, Hitler ordered the army back into this zone, and all schools, including my *Gymnasium*, were turned out to cheer the entering troops. The enthusiasm of older spectators was less marked, as many cast an anxious eye skywards to see whether Allied bombers were coming on a punitive raid.

My father always maintained that this first major foreign policy success of Hitler's resulted, straight away, in a considerable tightening of the bonds in which the Nazis held Germany. Certainly, we as a family would probably have found it impossible to leave Germany as easily as we did in April 1936 had we waited any longer. We took with us most of our possessions. These were loaded into containers as we packed up, under the supposedly strict supervision of a customs officer, who allowed me to play with his sealing pliers while he drank endless cups of coffee, supplied by my mother.

We flew from Frankfurt to Berlin in a Lufthansa JU 52, the civilian version of the plane which, three years later, was one of the mainstays of the Luftwaffe as a transport aircraft and as a bomber. We then travelled from Berlin to Hamburg in the 'Flying

Hamburger', the crack express of the German state railways. I believe that the record time for this journey was only equalled some years after the reunification of Germany, when the railway network ceased to be divided into a West and an East German network. From Hamburg, we travelled to Bremerhafen where we boarded the transatlantic liner, *Bremen*, for the thirty-hour journey to Southampton. The complicated method of travel was due to the need to conserve as much foreign currency as possible, our German marks not being freely convertible into pounds sterling.

Schooldays in London and Birmingham, 1936–1942

Our new lives commenced in May 1936, when the *Bremen* docked in Southampton, close to the almost-completed *Queen Mary*, which later broke the *Bremen's* record for the fastest transatlantic crossing.

I was enormously impressed by the sight of the thousands of identical-looking brick houses, each with its smoke-belching chimney, as the boat train steamed into Waterloo Station.

A taxi took us to our hotel, via East Carriage Drive, where we overtook a column of hunger marchers, seemingly shepherded by one lone policeman. With memories of street fights between the police and Nazis or Communists on marches in Germany still fresh in our minds, we found this early introduction to British law and order very exciting.

The summer of 1936 passed like a flash for all of us, and a great deal was achieved. My parents settled on West Dulwich as a place to live, convenient by fast train to Victoria station for my father's office, off Victoria Street, and convenient for me for Dulwich College, where I was to go as a day-boy in the autumn, if I could pass the Common Entrance examination. They found a house, which cost £1,000, unpacked the furniture and engaged an English maid, who was able to introduce my mother to the mysteries of a black-leaded kitchen range and of open, coal-burning fireplaces in every room.

That summer, I was sent to a coaching establishment in Eastbourne, where I passed quickly through the three stages of learning a language: the first stage, in which you can say whatever you want to, but do not understand a word of what is said to you, the second, in which you can understand what others say but cannot express yourself, and the final stage, where you can both speak and understand.

I have been told by a linguistic specialist that I was extremely fortunate in making the transition from speaking German as my principal language to speaking English at about the time of my twelfth birthday. Had I been a little younger, I would have forgotten much of my German and, had I been just a little older, I would not have lost my German accent.

As it is, I find that my experience is an illustration of the high proportion of the adult vocabulary and understanding that is complete at the age of twelve. I still find that I can read a German book, fiction or non-fiction, written before the last war almost as quickly as an English one and that I hardly ever need a dictionary. Of course, I often have to guess the meaning of later modern slang or technical terms. Now, after a few days, at most, in German surroundings, my spoken German is sufficiently fluent for most people not to guess that I am not a permanent German resident and speaker.

I find it difficult to answer a question that is often put to me: when was it my parents and I stopped speaking German to one another? I suppose it must have been at the outbreak of war, when it was not so terribly sensible to walk about in the blackout speaking German. At the same time my mother persuaded my father not to use his monocle, which made him look like the Prussian officer he had been in World War I.

My mother's English was fluent but she had an accent that sounded more Dutch than German. This was, and still is, common in anyone educated in Hamburg. My father spoke with an American accent, dating back to his time in Pittsburgh. It took him a little time to break himself of the habit of addressing every lady as ma'am.

I know that when I had been at Dulwich College for a year I preferred reading RL Stevenson's *Treasure Island* in English to reading it in a German translation. However, for Swift's *Gulliver's Travels*, I used my German translation as a crib. At the same time, Scott's *Ivanhoe* was a set book at school, which I found difficult, just as I found Shakespeare difficult. I have discovered no letters later than 1939 in German, either from me to my parents or from them to me.

I do not know whether my relative lack of appreciation of poetry in any language is the price I am paying for having changed languages. I find the metre of most German classical poetry wooden and uninteresting and I very rarely read English poetry for pleasure, whereas I greatly enjoy reading good English prose. Whether I can write it is for the reader to decide.

During some of my school holidays my mother read plays by Goethe, Schiller, Lessing, and other German classical writers with me. Music meant very little to my mother. As a girl she had been bored to tears whenever she was taken to the opera in Hamburg. My father's taste for music was limited to operatic arias, and he had quite a collection of Caruso and Gigli gramophone records. The first orchestral music I heard was when I saw Walt Disney's *Fantasia* in 1938. Although I came to know and enjoy classical music at Cambridge, I have never acquired the habit of, or the need for, listening regularly to music

I took the Common Entrance examination at Dulwich College, in the late summer of 1936 and was accepted into the Upper Third form, which was about right for my age. My main recollection of the examination is that I had never been asked to draw a sketch map before and probably made a hash of mine. In the general knowledge paper, not knowing how common sets of initials are in English, I wrote an eloquent account of the USSR when asked to say what I knew about the LCC. The correct answer would have been 'nothing', which would probably have given me even fewer marks.

The form master of the Upper Third was generally regarded as a terror, who frequently lost his temper and handed out detentions and other punishments in every lesson. However, to me, who was accustomed to the sadists of the German *Gymnasium*, he seemed meekness and mildness itself. He quickly realised that I was well in advance in Latin, French, and mathematics, and, when I came top of the form order at Christmas, he suggested that I should move up to the Modern Fourth form in January. This involved my sitting at the back of the form during elementary German lessons and teaching myself Spanish from a primer, which was not very satisfactory. Accordingly, at half term I was moved into the Classical Fourth form, which had already been doing Greek for a term and a half. With amazing elasticity and forbearance, the school arranged a private class in beginner's Greek for another latecomer and for me. We both caught up with the others by Easter which, in retrospect, does not say very much for their rate of progress, and joined them in the summer term. At the end of the school year, a small group, which included me, moved straight into the Upper Fifth, leaving out the Lower Fifth altogether.

The school year 1936–7 was indeed a momentous one for me. I had started the year in Germany; had then gone to school in Eastbourne and been in three different forms at Dulwich. I had learned to cope with the starched white collar of my school uniform, been introduced to the mysteries of rugby and cricket and had overcome the feeling of strangeness when swimming in the school swimming baths in the buff. Outside events impinged increasingly on everyone's consciousness: in addition to witnessing the remilitarisation of the Rhineland, we read with a mixture of vestigial pride and uneasy awe of German achievements in the Berlin Olympic Games. We also read of the end of the Italian conquest of Abyssinia, the start of the Civil War in Spain, and about Roosevelt's landslide second-term victory. We watched the Crystal Palace burn from our house in Dulwich. When my father went on a business trip to the Continent, he brought back news about the impending abdication of Edward VIII, which only reached British newspapers a week later. We watched the proclamation of George VI from St James's Palace.

The next school year was my School Certificate year, and I do not remember being particularly worried by the examination, nor were the four of us who were only fourteen particularly surprised at having obtained six credits, or in my case seven, with a gratuitous one in German. It was merely amusing to think that we had now satisfied the formal requirements for Oxford or Cambridge entry. At schools like Dulwich it was taken for granted that, if you were placed in the classical side and were in the top set in mathematics, you could go on to university if you wanted to, or rather, if your parents could pay the fees. It was very different from today's competition for places at universities, and from the rivalries between schools for their position in the league tables.

At that time there was a well-defined pecking order between the three sides of the school: the brightest boys were in the classical side and did Greek as well as Latin, the middle stream were in the modern side, where they learnt a second modern language in addition to French, and where they might also do some Latin. The science side, where there was no Latin and where one concentrated on physics and chemistry, was strictly for the weaker brethren. There was, however, a very progressive institution at Dulwich, known as the Science Remove, which was for those, like myself, who had had no science lessons at all and were then brought up to Higher School Certificate standard in physics and chemistry and in mathematics or biology (mainly for intending medical students) in two years. Even so, when I informed my form master that that was the form into which I wanted to go, he said: 'But you do not have to do science; you are good enough to do Classics'. I have found that more than one of my colleagues who have become successful professional scientists have had similar experiences at school.

In fact, I did not benefit very much from the Science Remove at Dulwich. The autumn of 1938 was that of the Munich crisis and, in the expectation of war and intense aerial bombardment of London, half of Dulwich College was evacuated to the wilds of the Forest of Dean in Gloucestershire. We were accommodated in a disused miners' quarantine isolation camp for two weeks until Neville Chamberlain returned from his talks with Hitler, promising 'Peace in our Time'.

My father did not share in the fairly widespread relief at the time but considered the attempts at appeasement a political disaster. He was very proud later of having said to a neighbour, a staunch supporter of the Liberal Party, that the only British politician who understood the danger from the dictators was Winston Churchill, and that he should become Prime Minister. He was told that he still did not understand England; Churchill could never become the head of the British government as he was far too unreliable.

On our return from the Forest of Dean, I only had a few more weeks at Dulwich. My father had negotiated the sale of his agency to the Birmingham company, W & T Avery, and our family moved to Birmingham after Christmas. My parents were strongly prejudiced against British boarding schools, which on the Continent were widely regarded as sinks of iniquitous homosexual practices. Accordingly, I was sent to the King Edward VI

School in Birmingham, which had nothing resembling the Dulwich Remove and where I had to join a class where everyone had studied physics and chemistry for School Certificate. For the first time in my school career, I had to struggle to keep up.

During the first weeks in Birmingham, we stayed in a residential hotel. My mother, against all regulations, had smuggled our cat into our hotel room. One day, having emptied the contents of the cat's litter tray into a paper bag, she furtively took it down to the bin clamped to a lamppost at the bus stop outside the hotel. Having disposed of her burden, she was about to board a bus when a heavy hand at the end of a blue-clad arm descended on her shoulder and she was asked to explain the contents of her parcel to the constable. When she confessed to a crime less heinous than those perpetrated by the IRA, who were going through a period of leaving bombs in public places, the policeman released her only after he had very gingerly unwrapped her parcel to check her truthfulness.

From the hotel, we moved into a large rented Victorian semi-detached house in Edgbaston. The other half of the house was occupied by the family of Professor, later Sir, Rudolf Peierls, then professor of applied mathematics at Birmingham University, and his lodgers. These were, in turn, Otto Frisch and Klaus Fuchs. Two years later, we shared the cellars of the house, which had been converted into an air raid shelter, during the more than one hundred nights of successive air raids on Birmingham. I cannot claim that my resolve to become a research physicist was in any way the result of the concentration of physicists next door: Peierls and Frisch drafted the 1940 memorandum on the feasibility of constructing an atomic bomb there and Fuchs became infamous as the 'atom spy'. We were, of course, ignorant of all the goings-on next door until very much later. We merely heard Mrs Peierls' explanations of her husband's wartime journeys to the United States as having something to do with his 'Rabbit Machine', her code word for the atomic bomb, as we guessed later.

When war came in 1939, King Edward's School was evacuated to Repton in Derbyshire. The sixth-formers, of whom I was now one, were billeted in outlying villages. I landed in a fairly primitive farm, some five miles from Repton, from where I had to commute to school by bicycle. For me, as for many people who were evacuated or had to receive evacuees, the experience was a social education. I had never lived in a house without running water, electricity or indoor toilets. Many of the older villagers still knuckled their foreheads to members of the family at the 'Big House'. They had forgotten most of the meagre school learning that they had received long ago. When we all had to register for our National Registration identity cards, my offer to fill in the form for them was greeted with relief by my hosts who were not so very happy when they were required to write much more than their names. Even though they could not understand my always wanting to be at my books and my other strange ideas, they were kind and friendly hosts. I enjoyed being taken ferreting but did not show great enthusiasm for learning to milk the cows.

When no enemy bombing attacks materialised during what became known as the 'phoney war', we could go home for the Christmas holidays to a, so far, unscathed Birmingham. It was quite a hardship when I had to go back to my village of Ticknall, especially as a really arctic winter had set in early in 1940. A heavy fall of snow made the road to Repton impassable and, after a while, I set off on foot for Burton-on-Trent, where I caught a train for home. I spent more than three weeks in urban comfort and, when I returned to Derbyshire, my absence from school had not even been noticed.

Fortunately, the hardships of winter induced many boys to leave Derbyshire permanently so that, after Easter, space became available in the boarding house in Repton for those of us about to take Higher School Certificate. The last weeks of revision were accompanied by the dreadful news from the Continent, where the German army was racing through the Low Countries and into France. In sadness we stuck pins into a large map to show the position of the Front, but when a boy who was preparing himself to read history at Oxford, turned back from the map and said, 'We have lost the war', he was greeted with nothing but derision. The first examination paper coincided with the first air raid warning but no bombs fell near Repton. The last paper was just before the fall of France. The school decided to return to Birmingham and, though the start of the next school year signalled the beginning of frequent air raids on the city, it proved to be the right decision.

I myself had reason to be grateful for the successive moves from Ticknall to Repton and from there to Birmingham which probably saved me from internment. I was now over sixteen and technically an 'Enemy Alien'. By the time I again had a settled address at home the policy of wholesale internment had been abandoned. It caught, among many others, my friend Peter Trier who was taken and, briefly, sent to a camp in Canada, in spite of the fact that the Nazis had murdered his father. My father was exempt by virtue of his job and, presumably, because his application for naturalisation was in the pipeline.

At sixteen, I was still too young to go to university and I decided to spend another year at school to prepare myself for a Cambridge scholarship and get better grades than I had obtained in my first, rather mediocre, efforts at the Higher School Certificate.

The start of the school year coincided with the beginning of the nightly air raids. At first we made our way to the reinforced cellar in our 'siren-suits', shapeless felt overalls, every time there was an alert. We tried to sleep on straw-filled paliasses. Fortunately, our part of Birmingham remained relatively unscathed, although we had a few windows broken by the blast from nearby bomb explosions and an incendiary bomb burnt out harmlessly in the garden. We could see the glow of fires on the horizons all around us, especially in the east during the savage raid on Coventry, but we were very lucky and soon stayed in our beds unless the aerial activities became very fierce. One such night my father ushered us into the shelter. When we emerged after the all clear my parents' bedroom window was broken and a piece of shrapnel was embedded in my father's pillow. The shrapnel was later ground into a letter opener that I use to this day. School went on pretty normally; there were few daytime alerts, and I do not think that any of my school friends were bombed out. Each bomb affected a relatively small region, compared with the total area of the city, and the devastation in residential areas was much less than in or near special targets such as docks or closely-packed industrial areas.

Part of my journey to school was spent in the rattling double-decker trams which, after dark, were less likely to go astray in the blackout than the buses, whose headlamps were masked but for a minute area. Thick netting was glued to the insides of the windows of all public transport vehicles. It was supposed to prevent injuries from flying shards of glass in case of a nearby bomb explosion. It was hard to resist the temptation to pick at the netting. London Transport gave advice with the help of a busy-body cartoon character called Billy Brown of London Town who, in one drawing, admonished a peeler with the words: 'I trust you'll pardon the correction; that stuff is there for your protection'.

I was with my father one day when the tram seemed to be going faster than usual downhill. The driver had fainted and collapsed over the speed-control wheel. The conductor panicked and jumped off the platform, shouting, 'We'll overturn at the bend at the bottom of the hill!' My father calmly leant out of the back window, seized the cable coming from the dolly and pulled it off the overhead wire and then applied the brake. As he refused to give his name, the story never found its way into the papers.

My parents and I were very regular theatregoers. Birmingham had two very good repertory theatres, the Birmingham Repertory Theatre and the Alexandra Theatre. There was thus a very varied programme of the older plays by Oscar Wilde and George Bernard Shaw and of more recent plays by J.B. Priestley, Somerset Maugham, and others. There was always the added interest with the repertory companies of seeing what part one's favourite actors would be playing that week.

More ambitious productions were put on by touring companies at the Theatre Royal. I remember seeing Ivor Novello in *Lilac Time*, Irving Berlin in a patriotic Anglo-American production, and the touring company from Covent Garden in *Löhengrin* and in *The Meistersinger*.

During the war we tried to make our evening visits into town on moonlit nights. In the dark it was quite difficult to recognise one's destination bus stop, even on routes with which one was completely familiar.

Travelling by train in wartime always presented problems. Seats were always difficult to find and the time of one's arrival was uncertain. When, in 1942, I went up to Cambridge, I had two choices for the journey between Cambridge and Birmingham: either I could take three separate trains, with long waits at the interchange stations, or I could travel via London, which I preferred. One never quite knew during the journey where one had got to; all station names had been removed to make things more difficult for a possible invading army. The Birmingham firm of cleaners called Beckets of Birmingham had over-painted their delivery vans with the legend 'Beckets of you know where'.

At school my exact generation was fortunate in the people who taught us, especially in the sciences. Many of our teachers had left their universities at the time of the Depression. They had been forced into school teaching as there was a great scarcity of the research jobs into which they would have loved to have gone and which they inspired us to desire for ourselves.

I enjoyed my last year at school, not only because of the interest of the physics and chemistry and mathematics syllabuses, but also because I made two friends with whom I shared a lot of interests. Jim Hackforth-Jones was as voracious a reader of books as I was and it was a great joy to have someone with whom I could discuss my latest discoveries. We remained close friends until his untimely death in a car accident some thirty years later. We were at Cambridge together, he was the best man at my wedding, and his daughter Toria, my goddaughter, was a bridesmaid. Toria married Christoph Viebahn, now a professor of anatomy at Göttingen University in Germany, who was educated at the same *Gymnasium* in Darmstadt that I had attended. I have had many enjoyable visits from the delightful Viebahn sons, who are the fifth generation of the Hackforth-Jones family I have known.

At school, we used surnames or nicknames among ourselves and I can well remember my acute embarrassment when I first met Jim's parents and grandmother and had to address him as 'Jim' instead of 'Hack' in front of his family.

My other classmate at school who became a lifelong friend was Morrin Acheson. His eccentric Irish doctor father encouraged Morrin's interest in chemistry and helped him to equip a laboratory in their garden shed that had much better facilities than the school's. Here, Morrin carried out complicated and, at times, dangerous, chemical syntheses. He later became a distinguished organic chemist at Oxford and a fellow of Queen's College. He has now retired to Switzerland, where he runs the cantonal bird protection society in fluent Swiss German with a strong Irish accent.

Higher School Certificate came and went as the Germans invaded Russia and this time I performed more creditably. Unfortunately for the state of the family finances, I was still stateless and not a British subject and so not eligible for a State Scholarship, which I would have won with my marks. So I entered for a college scholarship at St John's College, Cambridge to be taken up the following year. To fill in the time, I enrolled at Birmingham University for a year. I joined numerous clubs and societies, learnt to drink beer and smoke a pipe, and went to weekly dances in the students' union, but otherwise did not get a great deal of benefit from the lectures. Like many others who had been prepared for a university scholarship in a good school I found that I had done about eighty per cent of the first year syllabus in physics, mathematics, and chemistry and did not have the sense to realise how important the remaining twenty percent was.

I continued my own private tradition of sitting an important examination at the same time as a momentous event in the war. The Cambridge scholarship examination took place as the Japanese attacked Pearl Harbor. Two and a half years later, I was to sit the last paper of the tripos on D-Day, the Allied invasion of the Continent.

I fell in love with Cambridge. Even on freezing cold days in a winter fog and the wartime blackout Cambridge had a mystical quality. During the days of the scholarship examinations, I met again a number of my Dulwich contemporaries. To our mutual surprise, we had all more or less reached our adult height and I was no longer the smallest of my peers. I did not win a scholarship, or even get a place, at St Johns but, on the strength of my performance in the scholarship papers, Edward Welbourne, the somewhat eccentric senior tutor of Emmanuel College, accepted me to read natural sciences in the autumn of 1942.

I spent the summer of that year in the analytical laboratory of my father's firm of W & T Avery in Birmingham. During the temporary absence of the senior chemist of the laboratory, I did all the routine analyses. I found it easy and the industrial experience was useful, but finished the time there in the hope that I should be able to find a more challenging and interesting job after graduating. I was left with a dislike for clocking in and out and for other features of a job in industry.

Undergraduate years in Cambridge, 1942–1944

In October 1942, I came up to Emmanuel College to read natural sciences: physics, chemistry, mathematics, and electronics. The last of these subjects was compulsory for anyone reading science and was intended to prepare us for wartime jobs in radio communication and radiolocation (later known as radar). There was great demand in the services, and in civilian positions, for people trained in electronic engineering. The electronics course was taught in collaboration with the staff of Queen Mary College, London, which had been evacuated to Cambridge from its Mile End Road home. Other evacuees from London were Bedford College, the London School of Economics and parts of King's College. This influx, mostly of women, contributed greatly to the social life of Cambridge.

I was fortunate to be given a ground floor room in college, as a result of my being enrolled in the college fire brigade. My room was soon in use as a cloakroom by people in my year in digs, but I had discovered its most important function on the first night of term when I was woken by the presence of several people who, one after the other, plunged through my wide-open window. At that time your name was entered in the gate book in the porters' lodge and you were fined if you came in after 11 p.m. Those in college rooms were not allowed to leave college after 10 p.m. Wooden blocks were screwed into the window frames of ground floor rooms that only allowed the sash windows to be opened by a small amount. A previous occupant had removed these blocks in my window, which was then one of the most frequently used entrances and exits after hours. The following winter someone foolishly climbed out that way after a slight snowfall and left footprints that were seen by the head porter. He sent Arthur, the college carpenter, round to my room to put in new blocks. He arrived while I was entertaining a young lady to tea and was happy to accept a large slice of cake. After he had finished, Arthur laid his ruler across the young lady's bosom and murmured: 'It will be a bit of a squeeze for you, madam, but I dare not leave you more than eighteen inches.' He did, and it was enough, just. Good relations with the college porters were, and remained, very important. We once had a highly illegal party in my room with several girls. Long after midnight, we made our way to the bathhouse, the roof of which had now become the preferred way for climbing in and out of college. In the cloisters we ran straight into the porter who was making his rounds and who shone his torch carefully up and down each member of the group. Finally, with a, 'Good evening, gentlemen', he switched off his torch and vanished into the shadows.

Twenty years later, as a married man with a family, I returned to Cambridge, and we bought a house in Little Shelford. We put a notice in the village post office advertising for someone to help in the house. In due course, a respectable lady turned up who said that for many years she had been cook for Mr Welbourne.

'You mean the master of Emmanuel?' asked Valerie. 'He was my husband's tutor when he was an undergraduate.'

The respectable lady said she would let us know about the job and only agreed to come to us after, as she told us later, having consulted her brother, who had been a porter at Emmanuel and who, after looking me up in his diary, reported that I was a nice quiet gentleman whose wife would probably be a suitable employer for his sister. It was he who had wielded the torch.

During the war we had breakfast, lunch, and dinner in Hall and surrendered our ration books to the buttery. In return, we could draw half a jam jar of sugar, and our diminutive butter, margarine, and marmalade or jam rations for consumption in our rooms. In those days, before laundrettes and before washing machines for the use of undergraduates, I sent my washing home in a lockable wicker basket fitted with a reversible address label. The clean washing came back to Cambridge, usually accompanied by a cake or some other delicacy.

On the whole, college meals were not too bad, but they were not very good either. Having all our meals in common probably gave us more social coherence as a college than is usual in normal peace time. Added to that was that there were few undergraduates from either a very wealthy or a very poor family background. A high proportion of us had been to good grammar or minor public schools. There was little swank or snobbery and we all had to work hard. Deferment from call-up was only granted to natural scientists, engineers, and medical students, and then only for two years. A third class in one's first year examination usually terminated one's academic career automatically. As a result of all this, we were a pretty happy community, and I can only remember a few misfits who were unhappy at Emmanuel.

One such unfortunate was a major scholar in mathematics, who came from an Ebbw Vale mining family. At school he had always been the one who was head and shoulders above the rest of his class. He felt it very severely that, at Cambridge, his abilities were no more than average when compared with his peers. One of the least popular pastimes was to have to 'volunteer' to wash up after Hall in the fairly unsanitary kitchen. My Welsh friend volunteered frequently, feeling more at home with the college servants than with his contemporaries. He was, of course, rebuffed, the college servants being much greater snobs than the undergraduates. He only got a third class in the end-of-year exam and disappeared from the scene.

Towards the end of the summer term, I found myself remarking to the college butler in front court that it seemed to be a very popular time for visits from one's people.

'Oh yes sir,' he said, 'and you can always tell from the sort of people a gentleman has what kind of a gentleman a gentleman is.'

In 1945, when I was doing 'war research' – about which I shall write more later – I arrived back at the college gates, together with Frank Dobie, the first visiting professor of American history. We had both been to a meeting addressed by Emmanuel Shinwell, a very left wing Labour MP. At the gate we met Freestone, the head porter.

'Have you been to hear Mr Shinwell?' asked Dobie.

'Oh no, sir. I am a staunch supporter of the Conservative Party,' said Freestone, to the surprise of Professor Dobie, who obviously felt that a working man should be a Labour voter.

Politics and political societies played an important part in Cambridge life. The most important club was CUSIA, the Cambridge University Society for International Affairs. I never knew of anyone who attended their, no doubt very interesting, lectures but large numbers of us flocked to the CUSIA Thursday tea dances at the, alas long-defunct, Dorothy Café. The Union played a much smaller role than in peacetime, but I rarely missed the weekly debate organised by the Emmanuel College Debating Society, of which, in due course, I became secretary and vice-president.

The debates were conducted in parliamentary style: all speeches had to be addressed to the chair and there was always a proposer and a seconder of the motion and a proposer with a seconder for the opposition. After their speeches, the debate was thrown open to the floor. Subjects alternated between serious political ones: 'This house believes that a Second Front should be opened now'; 'The second chamber in Parliament should be elected' and the facetious ones: 'Men are clay and women make mugs of them'; 'Englishmen can make decisions by instinct, without having to think'.

The last of these was a motion for the Dons' Debate. It was proposed by the senior tutor, Edward Welbourne, whose argument was that there were no Englishmen, which thesis he proceeded to defend by reading out the names of speakers at meetings from posters in the debating chamber, most of whom had non-English names. We waited to see how he would deal with the largest poster, which advertised a lecture by one John Smith. According to Welbourne, this name was obviously fictitious and he was really an Armenian with an unpronounceable name. This view was apparently shared by the Metropolitan Police, who took the name of the distinguished biochemist John Smith, when he was an innocent bystander at the Notting Hill Carnival, and hauled him off to the police station for giving a false name.

As secretary of the debating society, I had charge of its correspondence file and was amused to find that only a few years earlier Emmanuel had invited Girton College to a joint debate. In her letter of acceptance, their secretary inquired whether Emmanuel could provide a chaperone or whether Girton had to bring one along. The college debates taught me a lot. I have never since been seriously afraid of joining in scientific discussions or other meetings.

Although quite unmusical myself, I was exposed to a good

deal of music at Emmanuel, partly through the weekly musical evenings held by the dean, the Rev. Hugh Burnaby, the mild-mannered clerical member of a family that included at least one well-known actor. At one of the musical evenings, Bobby Fisher, the youngest son of the then archbishop of Canterbury, had his request for a song refused by the dean, whereupon Bobby threatened to denounce the dean to his father.

'Your father, my dear Fisher, has no authority whatsoever over the dean and chaplain of a Cambridge college,' was the firm reply. I have never discovered how that independence was achieved.

Undergraduates, when out after dark in Cambridge, were obliged to wear academic dress, which then included cap as well as gown. Academic caps (mortar boards) were a favourite trophy for American soldiers who started to arrive in England in large numbers. The trick was for a car to draw up next to an under-graduate in cap and gown with a mumbled request for directions. When the undergraduate leant forward politely to hear the question more clearly, an arm would shoot out and grab the cap and the car would drive off with a squealing of tyres. I must have been among the last people to be 'progged' (caught by a proctor) for failing to wear a cap after dark. The American tactics made the enforcement of the cap regulation impossible after my first term.

The proctor was accompanied by two constables ('bulldogs'), who were reputedly selected for their running ability at the annual sports day of the university assistants' club. The proctor had the right to send any junior member (undergraduate) of the university back to college if he was walking arm-in-arm with an unsuitable female companion. An old story reports the following dialogue:

Proctor: Excuse me, sir, are you a member of the university?

Undergraduate: Yes, sir.

Proctor: Would you please introduce me to your, hmm, lady friend?

Undergraduate: Yes, sir, but this is not my lady friend; she is my sister.

Proctor: Are you aware of the fact, sir, that your, hmm, sister has a rather unsavoury reputation in this town and university?

Undergraduate: Yes sir, I know. Dad is awfully het up about that.

One of the traditional Cambridge sports, against which the

proctors had been fighting for generations, was night climbing. There were many popular ascents of college and university buildings, whose relative severity was frequently debated. The sceptre in the hands of King Henry VIII above Trinity Great Gate had been exchanged for a chair leg so often that the latter was left in place and merely painted over in gold paint. Night climbing was made almost respectable by the activities of the college fire brigades, whose practice sessions every week gave official approval to making our way along the roof to lookout points built for spotting fires started by incendiary bombs. We also practised abseiling from the tops of buildings. Our unit had a lethal three-section expanding ladder; it was much more dangerous to erect this monster and to prevent it from falling over than to climb up a drainpipe. We also competed in teams against one another to set records in connecting our hoses to standpipes or to our petrol engine-driven trailer pump. Often we finished up drenched, but we never had a fire to deal with in earnest. Indeed, no bombs fell on Cambridge after 1942.

Undergraduate and dons' politics in Cambridge were, on the whole, left of centre. The Conservative and Liberal Associations had a much lower profile than the two left wing clubs, the orthodox Labour Club, whose members were mostly card carrying members of the Labour Party, and the much more radical Cambridge University Socialist Club, with many communists among its members. These clubs were serious business for intending professional politicians, who regarded them as steppingstones in their careers.

I have found it interesting to observe the career of my Emmanuel contemporary, Donald Chapman, later Lord Northfield. Coming from an orthodox Yorkshire Labour Party background, he might have been expected to join the Labour Club, but he found it more advantageous to be the respectable face of the Socialist Club communists. Having been president of CUSC, he became a Cambridge city councillor and the 1945 general election agent for Major Symonds, who was elected as the first Labour MP for Cambridge, a success which owed a good deal to the canvassing efforts of Donald's CUSC friends.

I became somewhat disillusioned by the Socialist Club when I started to suspect that the results of the committee elections had been a little 'improved' to secure the return of candidates desired by the outgoing committee. In any case, I found informal conversations with a few friends over a cup of coffee or a glass of beer after Hall preferable to organised meetings. My friend Jim had preceded me to Emmanuel and was the focus of a group of congenial souls whom I enjoyed joining for arguments about all subjects under the sun, but mainly about Life with a capital 'L'.

One member of this group was Tony Fisher, who was to become a life-long friend. He was a Czech citizen, but having been brought up as a child in Vienna, coming to England after the *Anschluss*, he spoke very little Czech and had no desire to serve with the émigré Czech forces in England. When he received his call-up papers they had a minor misspelling of his name and so he wrote on the envelope, 'Not known at this address', returned it to the Czech recruiting office in London, and volunteered for the British Army before the Czechs caught up with him. At the end of the war, Tony served with AMGOT (Allied Military Government of Occupied Territories), where he met Eve, a Girtonian, whom he married. For a short while he was mayor of Aachen.

Another member of our group was an ardent Roman Catholic apologist. The philosophical approach of the Catholics appealed much more to many of us who did not feel at home with the evangelical muscular Christianity preached by CICCU, the Cambridge Intercollegiate Christian Union. I once came back to my room to find a note from an old acquaintance who had become vicar of Toft, a village near Cambridge, and who was a prominent senior member of CICCU. He said that he was fire watching in the crypt of Holy Trinity Church. I climbed out of my window and found him in the crypt. I apologised for being late, as I had been to a dance. I was soon on my knees praying with him to repent my sin of fondling strange women while clutching them during godless modern dances.

I see that I have described many activities but have not mentioned lectures, supervisions, and practical classes. Doing three subjects: physics, chemistry, and electronics, each involving practical classes, in addition to mathematics, filled my timetable pretty completely from 9 a.m. to 4 p.m., with supervisions to be fitted in before Hall. The most enjoyable lectures in optics and properties of matter, were by Alex Wood, a fellow of Emmanuel, who had the most entertaining repertoire of lecture experiments. It was great fun seeing his demonstration of the conservation of angular momentum, in which the old man was whirled round and round on a piano stool and then accelerated and decelerated as he brought two heavy steel balls in his hands closer to and further away from his body.

The practical physics laboratory was in the hands of GFC Searle, who enjoyed his reputation as a Cambridge character, and who had come back from retirement at the outbreak of war, not, I suspect, to the unmixed delight of his colleagues, none of whom, not even Professor Sir Lawrence Bragg, was safe from his, at times, very acid tongue.

Searle had invented practical physics as a university subject in the dark ages and had gone on inventing it ever since. In one of the many stories about him, he was doing a magnetometer experiment when he shouted across the laboratory to a woman student: 'You over there: are you wearing corsets? If so, take them off: every time you walk past, you make my magnetometer give a kick!' There were Searle's apparatus for measuring elastic constants, for determining the acceleration due to gravity, and for finding the surface tension of a soap solution by blowing a bubble; this last apparatus carried a notice:

> Students must use the bellows provided and not their foul, tobacco-laden breath to inflate the apparatus.

One of Searle's tricks was to hand out manuscripts describing new experiments involving long pages of calculations and to cackle with delight when the recipient had failed to spot deliberate mistakes in the mathematics. I found two such errors and thereafter had difficulties avoiding being used as a guinea pig to try out ever more elaborate new experiments. I attended Searle's eightieth and eighty-fifth birthday parties in the Cavendish Laboratory in 1944 and 1949.

Electronics was also fun and acquainted many of us for the

first time with modern instruments such as cathode-ray oscillo-scopes. I do not think that many budding physicists guessed how much of their future work would be dominated by electronic techniques. At the outbreak of war, when experts in the design of very sensitive amplifiers were needed, they were more likely to be found in university departments of physiology than of physics.

The chemistry classes were very large and, for some strange reason, often rather unruly. I disliked organic chemistry as being too smelly, and inorganic chemistry, as I was somewhat colour blind and could never see the end-point colour change in the titrations in volumetric analyses.

Mathematics was interesting, but rather hard work. I did not realise until my second year that, in mathematics, I could not coast along on the basis of what I had done at school; I was now learning new things, which required much real thought.

On the strength of my marks in physics and electronics in the preliminary examination for part I of the natural sciences tripos, I was one of the minority who, in our second year, was allowed to work for part II of the tripos, so that we could drop chemistry, and any other subjects that we might have been taking, to concentrate on our main subject only, which in my case was physics. The majority of my contemporaries continued with three full subjects and took part I of the tripos at the end of their second year and left with the qualifications for a general science degree. Many of them came back to Cambridge for one year after the war to take part II of the tripos. Only women were allowed a third year: some of them spent two years on part I and the third on part II. This had been the normal practice before the war for many, if not most, scientists.

The long-term outlook for the family finances was somewhat parlous, especially as my father's health was not very good. It seemed very doubtful that I would be able to come back to Cambridge at a later date to take part II of the tripos if I contented myself with sitting only the preliminary examination to part II. This would also have qualified me for a war-time degree, but I now decided to take the tripos examination itself, instead of the preliminary examination. This amounted to staking everything on one card: one could only sit for a tripos examination once and, if I failed in this, I would be left with nothing. The course was a very tough one and, in addition, it was tempting to sit in on some of the lectures given by the great ones of modern physics. Eddington was still lecturing on general relativity and Dirac on quantum mechanics. Both started their lecture courses in the largest theatre in the arts school, and both continued in smaller rooms. I do not believe that either was aware of his audience shrinking, or indeed appeared to know or care that he had an audience. As the year went on, I cut down quite a bit on lectures, and instead used the time to read the relevant textbooks. I have never found lectures a very efficient way of absorbing information, especially in mathematical subjects, where one can really only understand the derivations fully by working through each step on paper. It was only later, when I was giving supervisions myself, that I discovered that I had learnt some proofs and solutions by rote without fully understanding what I was doing.

I was very fortunate in having an excellent supervisor in Tony French of Sidney Sussex College. He was able to help me with most of my queries and problems as they arose. For the more esoteric questions he wanted a week's notice to prepare a lucid explanation. I only realised how good he had been on any branch of physics when he insisted that during the summer term I should go to an eminent nuclear physicist. When I asked the great man about a problem I had in thermodynamics, he said to me: 'My dear Arndt, you are fortunate to have for a supervisor someone who is an international authority on nuclear physics. Do not waste your time and mine by asking me about other branches of physics.' I was, at first, very impressed, but later I had some unworthy thoughts and, when I gave supervisions myself, I used this ploy myself to good effect.

During the course of the year, the nuclear physicists in the Cavendish mostly disappeared to secret destinations in Canada and in the United States. I have heard it said that one of our lectures was the subject of a Cabinet decision: the question was whether it was more suspicious to give the normal lecture on nuclear fission, without, of course, any reference to the atomic bomb project, or to drop it quietly (the lecture, not the bomb), in case the contents of undergraduate lectures were monitored by enemy agents. The lecture took place. In fact, I suspect that most of us had a shrewd suspicion that work on an atomic bomb was in progress, but I do not remember ever discussing the subject openly.

As a member of the college fire brigade, I was allowed to stay in college without charge during the vacations and I spent most of them in Cambridge, reading in the university library. During the Easter vacation, my father had to undergo a serious operation in Birmingham, and I decided to bicycle the hundred miles from Cambridge to visit him, which I succeeded in achieving in about nine hours. For the return trip, I was fortunate to have the company of my friend, Morrin Acheson, who decided to visit Cambridge before the beginning of his Oxford term. I do not know how many bomber aerodromes there were in the last flat miles, west of Cambridge, but as we cycled there was an almost continuous stream of bombers not very far above our heads. That night saw the first of the thousand bomber raids on Germany.

Our timetable had provision for almost two complete days of practical classes. The experiments were interesting and, no doubt, instructive but I felt that I could not afford the time to do many of the experiments properly and to write them up in the approved manner in a practical notebook. Quite often I looked at the instructions for the experiment, inspected the apparatus, and attempted to understand the theory and then went back to my reading. This amounted to taking another risk: at the end of the year, one handed in one's practical notebook and, if one had made a mess of the practical examination set for tripos, one could gain a few marks for a neat notebook.

In the event, I had much more luck than I deserved. The day before the practical exam, which took place on D-Day, the day of the Allied invasion of France, I realised that I had not revised the theory of either viscous flow of gases through a narrow tube or the surface tension of soap films, so I did some last minute cramming. The next morning, when I looked at the exam paper there were the almost unbelievable instructions:

> Blow a soap bubble at the end of the capillary tube provided. By timing the rate of collapse of the bubble as the air inside it escapes through the tube determine the surface tension of the soap film

and the viscosity of moist air.

There were only four third-year women and one other man who were taking the tripos examination, and, as a result of the extraordinarily lucky revision, I was the only one able to work out the theory of the experiment and then to get reasonable results for the viscosity of the air and the surface tension of the soap film. The others all had to get help from the examiners and lost marks because of the amount of information they had received. The exam lasted for six hours and only when we emerged at the end of it were we able to take in the momentous events, which had been taking place.

Some months later, Professor Sir Lawrence Bragg, who had been chief examiner for the practical and was not known for writing glowing testimonials, supported my application for naturalisation in the words, 'This country needs good scientists, especially scientists of unusual ability as experimentalists.' Thus I owe both my British nationality and my entire research career to a lucky fluke!

I only achieved a lower second class but the other man got a third. One of the women had an upper second, but women, at that time, were not members of the university, so that I can claim that I had the best physics tripos result of any member of the university that year.

Research student, 1944–1949

With examinations behind me, the question of my future now arose. Like all undergraduates, I had been summoned to appear before the university Joint Recruiting Board and had been interviewed by CP Snow, the novelist, at that time a fellow of Christ's College. I had expressed my preferences for a job connected with radio or radiolocation – now called radar – in the services, or failing that, in the merchant navy. That was turned down as I would have been too great a security risk and instead I was offered the choice between the Pioneer corps and a civilian research job. Not surprisingly, I chose the latter and had the gall to ask Sir Lawrence Bragg whether there were any war research jobs going in the Cavendish. He thought that there might be a vacancy in the crystallographic laboratory, which was then run by Henry Lipson, whom I had got to know and to like during my part II course. I was accepted to work on a project financed by the Electrical Research Association, which involved crystallographic and magnetic measurements on an alloy. This showed some promise for use as a permanent magnet material. If this work had been done five years earlier, and if it had been successful – which it was not – it might have led to the production of slightly better industrial magnets. The project was deemed to be a suitable one to lead to a research topic for a PhD when the war ended a year later.

Rather rashly, I decided that the X-ray techniques which were then in use in the department were not adequate for my purposes. I spent most of my time as a research student on the development of new techniques that I was to improve over many years. I was, in fact, quite unsuitable for the job for which I had been engaged as I had not even taken the part I course in mineralogy that would have given me the necessary background knowledge for X-ray crystallographic research. Fortunately, Lipson and his staff ran a summer school, mainly intended for people in industrial laboratories, which was a crash course in X-ray crystallography and which started shortly after the end of the summer term. So, within three weeks of having finished revising for my final examinations, I found myself working almost equally hard in acquiring a new subject.

The crystallography laboratory was part of the Cavendish laboratory (the university department of physics). Crystallography was somewhat removed from mainstream physics, which in the minds of Cambridge old-timers could only mean nuclear physics. We were a mixture of nationalities, having French, Belgians, Germans, Austrians, Canadians, Poles, and Hungarians in a group where the foreigners outnumbered the natives and we had a higher proportion of women than was then usual. There was a congenial atmosphere in the laboratory with lively discussions of politics and international affairs at the departmental tea table in the afternoon. Among the staff were Dennis Riley and Max Perutz, both of whom I was to have close contact with in my subsequent career.

I enjoyed the laboratory work, which I combined with giving supervisions to undergraduates and demonstrating in various teaching laboratories. One of the advantages of working in central Cambridge was that seminars and colloquia in other University departments were all within a few minutes' walk and, if one went out for coffee in the morning to the Copper Kettle or the Friar House, one was sure to meet people from other laboratories. A lot of these benefits have been lost by the dispersal of today's departments to the outskirts of Cambridge.

I was fortunate to be allowed to go on living in college and have my meals there, still thanks to my membership of the college fire brigade. Life was, of course, very different from what it had been during my undergraduate days. Most of my contemporaries had disappeared into the forces or into civilian war jobs. The few who remained, mainly medical students, had different timetables and different preoccupations from mine. I now had a little more time for non-scientific reading and made much use of Heffers' excellent second-hand book department. I wanted to keep up my French and bought many, almost disintegrated, second-hand French paperback detective stories. Amongst them was one entitled *Rien que ton corps* in which the *corps* turned out to be very definitely not a dead one. The book was spotted on my shelves by a South American student who thought that he had discovered in me a fellow enthusiast for *'zee pornographie'*.

I derived much pleasure from regular visits to the Arts Theatre in Cambridge. There were many excellent productions, especially in early 1945, when several major productions opened in Cambridge instead of the London West End while the V1s (doodle bugs) were falling on London.

The winters of 1944–5 and 1945–6 were very severe, and there was skating on the flooded field at the Newnham end of Granchester Meadows. Hot roasted chestnuts were on sale from a booth on a small island in the middle of the field. The thaw in 1946 saw severe flooding. On the night of the Newnham College Ball, the west side of Cambridge was cut off from the centre. Water was lapping over the top of Silver Street and Garrett Hostel Lane bridges (both these bridges have since been rebuilt with higher spans). A little way north of Milton, the road to Ely disappeared into a lake, which stretched as far as the outskirts of Ely.

College rooms have, of course, always been very cold. Trousers damp from the East Anglian drizzle and hung over a bedroom chair in the evening crackled with ice in the morning. In those days, there were no doors at the bottom of college staircases, and one had to lay a gown on the floor to stop up the gap under one's door, so that loose papers did not fly about. There was, of course, no central heating, and at times, the college was so short of coal that one could only light a fire in the minute grate on alternate days.

In the spring of 1945 came VE-Day, the end of the war in Europe, the sound of church bells and the end of the blackout that showed us an illuminated Cambridge, which my generation had never known. For our celebration, we took the college trailer pump and transferred it from its wheels to two lashed together punts and made a jet-propelled progress along the river.

The last duty of the college fire brigade was after the next Boat Club Bump supper, when a rope strung with chamber pots was slung across Front Court. We shot these pots down with high-pressure jets. In the middle of the proceedings a GI, loaded with cameras, wanted to know what was going on.

'We are having a fire brigade practice,' he was told.

'How often does this happen?'

'We have a practice once a week.'

I am afraid the American departed a firm opponent of lend-lease. But I also made friends with a corporal from Tallahassee who greatly enjoyed being shown round the lesser-known sights of Cambridge. When his unit packed up and went home he presented me with a box of photographic printing paper, which in due course was used for the diagrams in my PhD thesis.

August 1945 saw the landslide Labour election victory and the end of the war against Japan, after the dropping of the two atomic bombs on Hiroshima and Nagasaki. The existence of these bombs came as no great surprise to us, as I have described above.

Jim Hackforth-Jones had invited me for a week's sailing holiday in the Solent in his family's Lymington L-boat One-Design, to celebrate the restart of coastal sailing after VE-day. Beaulieu River was an almost continuous anchorage for leftover invasion landing craft and Yarmouth, Isle of Wight, was the main harbour for the motorboats of the Royal Army Service Corps, who were supplying the sea forts in those waters. It was almost as difficult to find a mooring there as it is these days during the summer bank holiday weekend.

With the end of the war, the atmosphere in Cambridge in general, and in the Cavendish laboratory in particular, underwent a radical change. Ex-service men, whose studies had been interrupted, started to trickle back and scientists returned from wartime jobs, many with completely new skills and fields of expertise. The impact was particularly great in the new subject of radio astronomy, where the experience gained in radar techniques led to immediate advances. But all experimental work benefited from the government surplus equipment, which was made available to university departments in huge quantities. We collected vast numbers of radio valves by the van load from dumps on airfields. The departmental vans were weighed on entry and on leaving and one paid a nominal charge per pound on the difference in weight. Not satisfied with the bargain prices, some people filled up their vans with scrap metal and old bedsteads, which they then dumped before reloading complete chassis of radar display electronics or precision gears, which had been part of gun-sight predictors. Adapting these wonderful components for use in research equipment was like playing with Meccano on a large scale and left a whole generation of physicists with a taste for building their own instruments, where their successors have been more inclined to plan their experiments around commercially available instrumentation.

Towards the end of 1945, the newly built Austin wing of the Cavendish laboratory was released from wartime research and we moved into luxurious premises, purpose-built for experimentation. When I built my first X-ray tube, it switched itself off very frequently. I wanted to be able to check from my room on the third floor when this had happened, so I connected an ammeter on my desk between the earth end of the high voltage transformer in the basement laboratory and the ground, via the pluggable internal wiring system, which allowed any room to be connected to any other via junction boxes on each floor. I had failed to connect a shunt resistor across the transformer terminals and, one day, someone pulled out the plug in the corridor and the voltage on the open socket rose to 50,000 volts. As he pulled, a long spark came out of the socket with the plug. Fortunately, he had the presence of mind to push the plug in again and so to extinguish the spark.

My research project also required electron microscope studies of my alloy samples. The American-made microscope was a lend-lease presentation to the Cavendish and was in the hands of a senior technician called Major Crow (the rank was the one he had held in the Home Guard). The electron microscope was not in the very best condition, needing a very complete overhaul and a careful cleaning of its interior. Two other research students and I volunteered to undertake the servicing of the instrument. The interior parts had to be taken out and washed in absolute alcohol and then in ether. The alcohol was, of course, quite pure enough for human consumption after it had been used; mixed with tonic water it was a good substitute for gin and tonic at the party we had to celebrate the re-commissioning of the microscope. When the instrument was working again, I proudly took the first photograph I had taken with it to Henry Lipson, who happened to be talking to Sir Lawrence Bragg and George Crow. Henry looked at the photo and said: 'Hmm, that is nothing to crow about, I mean, to brag about'. His sense of humour was not always appreciated.

I was very sorry when Henry Lipson left Cambridge to take up his new appointment as Professor of Physics at Manchester College of Technology and when Will Taylor became Reader in Crystallography at Cambridge and took over as head of the Laboratory of Crystallography and became my research supervisor. He never took much interest in what I was doing, in great contrast to Lipson, who was always on hand with help and advice.

Quite early on, I spoiled my relations with Taylor by what must have appeared to him like a colossal piece of impertinence on my part. I was in the lift with him and a visitor, whom he told that he must not forget to sign the visitors' book.

'So you still have security regulations?' asked the visitor.

'Oh no, just pleasant traditions and customs,' replied Taylor 'have we not, Arndt?'

I had a bad conscience over having spent rather a long time over coffee at the nearby Friar House that morning, and some devil made me say, 'Yes, such as having coffee in the morning and tea together in the afternoon.'

Taylor's face froze, and for several days afterwards he refused to acknowledge my existence. The explanation came when someone told me that I did not need to have a bad conscience over going out to coffee, since every day at 10.45 a.m. Taylor trooped out to the Copper Kettle with one of the women research students.

Somehow, I could not escape the subject of coffee with him. Several years later I was secretary of the X-ray Analysis Group of the Institute of Physics and Taylor was a committee member. We were discussing the programme of a forthcoming conference that we were organising and someone asked: 'What does your secretary think of the programme?'

'I do not think that we have allowed enough time for coffee,' I replied, and when I happened to catch Taylor's eye I knew what we were both thinking about at that moment.

Coffee was to continue to link my fate with Will Taylor's. Some fifteen years later, when I was working at the Laboratory of

Molecular Biology in Cambridge and when we, as a family of five, were living in Little Shelford, a village some three miles from Cambridge, Valerie found herself sitting next to Annie Taylor, Will's wife, at a coffee party. She mentioned that we were thinking of moving into Cambridge and had been looking at a house in Barrow Road, a few doors away from the Taylors, but that that had come to nothing. Annie told her that the owner of a house round the corner had just been appointed to a chair in Scotland and would be selling his house. We were successful in buying it and lived there happily for over thirty years. But it was always apparent that Will had much more neighbourly feelings towards Valerie than towards me.

With a return to peace time we were able to re-establish contact with our sole surviving close relatives, my uncle Ernst Juliusberg and his daughter Eva-Marie (Efje). They had survived the war reasonably well in Holland, but had gone very hungry during the last winter of the occupation. Efje came to stay with my parents in Birmingham for a few weeks for proper nourishment and a good rest (British rations were not as bad as some people have claimed). Efje had grown into a truly beautiful young woman. When she visited me in Cambridge for a few days, we had a wolf-whistling escort of all my friends and acquaintances wherever we went. She has spent all her life in The Hague, much occupied later with her family and her husband and his business affairs. I could never persuade her to come to England on another visit. I much enjoyed visiting them when, much later, I was making frequent business trips to Holland, but we were never really close. Observing how well my six grandchildren get on with one another, and how often they exchange visits, I realise how much I missed in not knowing my only living relative better.

But to return to my research work, I had conceived a wildly ambitious project, which involved building a new X-ray tube and an X-ray spectrometer of a then quite novel type. I did much of the construction work myself, relying of course, on government surplus equipment. I learnt some of the techniques I needed from unexpected teachers: I was doing some soldering and found that I was being observed with considerable disdain by the cleaning woman. When she could not stand my bumbling efforts any longer, she pushed me out of the way and showed me how to do a perfect job. She told me that she had worked for many years in the experimental canning department at Chivers' jam factory in Cambridge where she had soldered all the trial cans.

My instrument was far from complete when my grant finally came to an end and I had to leave Cambridge, having made only one set of highly dubious measurements. In fact, I continued to work on and off on some aspects of my self-imposed project for another fifty years.

I was again fortunate. Towards the end of my stay in Cambridge, Alan Wheeler and Wally Hall, then of the Birmingham University Department of Metallurgy, visited the Cavendish to make some X-ray measurements on Austenitic and Martensitic steels. They suggested that I joined them as a research fellow to collaborate with them in the construction of a proper X-ray powder spectrometer for their investigations of metal structures. Wally suggested a more convenient focusing method instead of the one that I had adopted. When I came to Birmingham, and we pooled our experience, we were very quickly able to assemble a precision Geiger counter spectrometer, which was a world first, as far as publication was concerned. We just beat the North American Philips Research Laboratories to it and probably deprived them of the possibility of patenting the similar instrument on which they were working.

The description of the instrument, and the discussion of the results that we obtained with it, rounded off my PhD thesis, which had so far seemed rather thin. My first nine months in Birmingham were rather hard; I worked in the lab during the day and on my thesis in the evenings until late at night. My mother typed the work and I produced the illustrations using the American photographic paper that I had been given by my American friend.

Finally, after months of toil the thesis was completed, bound and dispatched to Cambridge. My oral examination took place on a foggy November afternoon. I was very nervous of the outcome: my thesis was one of the first ones to come out of the crystallography department after the war and rumour had it that standards had been greatly raised. I was kept waiting for the examination for several hours and, when I was summoned to Will Taylor's office, it was quickly obvious that my examiners were not in a sunny mood. The external examiner was Professor Bill Astbury from Leeds, whose train had been severely delayed. He had refreshed himself on the way from his hip flask and he chain-smoked during the viva, thereby greatly annoying Will Taylor, the internal examiner, a non-smoker, who did not much like me in any case.

Will confined himself to questioning me in great detail about a theoretical point connected with my thesis. I discovered later that a paper discussing this question had been published in the latest issue of an American journal which had not yet arrived in Birmingham. Astbury asked me many questions along the lines of why had I done so-and-so instead of such-and-such and finally, what I considered to be the best part of my thesis. When I did not immediately answer he wanted to know of which part of my thesis was I particularly proud. Certain that all was lost, I could only reply that by that time I was no longer proud of any part of it.

'In that case,' said the examiners, 'we have no more questions to ask you.'

I was given no inkling of the outcome for about three months and, being certain of my failure, I was amazed to receive the good news that I was to be admitted to the degree of PhD at the next congregation in Cambridge. I now know that in scientific fields complete failures were rare and that usually the worst that happened to someone who had lasted the required three years was that he or she was made to rewrite parts of the thesis. Today's supervisor is very frequently the external examiner of the next pupil of today's examiner.

When I received my degree in the Senate House I was intrigued by the woman graduands in academic dress: women had become members of the university and now received Cambridge degrees instead of being 'invested with the title of the degree'. The long interval between Oxford and Cambridge admitting women as full members is usually explained by the fact that Cambridge is further to the east.

With more leisure, now that the thesis and two papers arising from it were completed, I enjoyed Birmingham more, but I was living with my parents in the small flat to which they had moved and I missed my independence and the companionship of contemporaries that I had had in Cambridge.

One of the people in the Birmingham metallurgy department whom I shall always remember was Maurice Jaswon, one of Alan Cottrell's research students, for demonstrating so clearly the different ways of thinking of a theoretician and an experimentalist. Maurice was an Irish Jew and I attributed his mathematical skills to the fact that he could use symbols from two alphabets – Hebrew and Eirse – unknown to most others, in his equations. His MSc project was to set up and solve rather intricate differential equations involved in the movement of dislocations in metal crystals. After many months, Maurice had found solutions to his equations and, good mathematician that he was, produced existence proofs of his solutions. Another couple of days would have been sufficient to insert numerical values in his equations and see whether they predicted the behaviour of real crystals correctly. But such a check did not interest Maurice: he had investigated a mathematically possible world and it was a very minor matter to him whether this world coincided with the real world or not. He went off on a well-deserved holiday and left the checks until his return.

I was again lucky in being offered a new job whenever I needed or wanted one. When I later told my daughter, Caroline, that I have never actually applied for a job, she said that that proved that I had no ambition whatsoever. Anyhow, just when I was beginning to feel that I had skimmed the cream off my metallurgical project, I ran into Dennis Riley, a former member of the Cambridge Crystallography Department, who was trying to build up a small team in the Davy-Faraday Laboratory of the Royal Institution in London, and he offered me a job there. One of the attractions was that the laboratory possessed the biggest X-ray tube in the world; it actually produced a much smaller intensity of useful X-rays than a standard small commercial X-ray tube but that was something I did not discover until later. The idea of working in such as prestigious place in the West End of London and perhaps living in a service flat like my friend Jim

Hackforth-Jones (oh, ultimate glamour!) appealed enormously and I accepted the offer more or less on the spot.

My father fell very seriously ill in the winter of 1949. When he did not appear to be recovering from an operation, it was decided that he should recuperate in a German sanatorium in the Black Forrest. His stay would be financed from some of my parents' restituted German funds, which had been confiscated by the Nazis during the war They had been recovered thanks to the efforts of a Hamburg lawyer who had been appointed by a court to represent my parents in their absence. He was completely unknown to them until after the war. It was one of the strange facts about the German legal system during the Nazi years that, while some appalling crimes were committed by some government departments, others functioned honestly and meticulously.

Two days before Christmas 1949, I accompanied my father on this, his last, trip. Arrangements were made for us to be collected at Frankfurt airport by a car, the driver of which had been my father's chauffeur in 1936. We were to be taken directly to the sanatorium in the Black Forest where my father was to recuperate while I stayed in a hotel a couple of miles away, allowing him to settle in. The journey developed quite differently from the plan. Just after we had taken off from the old Northolt Airport, fog closed down over northern Europe and, after what was obviously an anxious search for an airport that was still open, we landed at an RAF field near Hanover. We were fed in the warm officers' mess, where we waited until immigration officers from the nearest civilian airport had succeeded in battling their way by car through the fog. Our fellow passengers were driven in an open RAF lorry to Hanover Station to catch an all-night train to Frankfurt, but my father was obviously not capable of any more exertions that night. With the kind help of an AMGOT officer, I secured an air force Volkswagen Beetle to take us to a military hotel in Hanover. It was the first such car that we had seen since the much-trumpeted prototype, which had been shown in Darmstadt in 1935, and also the first heated car in which I ever travelled. After a night in a freezing hotel room, we were conveyed to a train and put into a sealed AMGOT coach to

Frankfurt. Our activities were rather complicated by the fact that we had no German currency (we would have been provided with funds by the driver who should have met us at Frankfurt). Any facilities belonging to the British Occupation Authority could only be paid for in BAFS (British Armed Forces money), of which we were only able to get a very small supply by changing a five pound note at the airport.

We were to find conditions in Germany very strange. The economic upswing, ushered in by the currency reform that had produced the Deutschmark, was gaining momentum. Coming from austere Britain, where severe rationing was still in force, we were amazed by the size of the meat portions in restaurants. While at home one had to plead to be allowed to buy more than one packet of cigarettes at a time, German tobacconists seemed to be amply stocked with all brands. These were all black market cigarettes, quite openly sold, in spite of the very occasional police raid and the subsequent fines, which were regarded as a normal trading expense.

Being in Germany was altogether a weird experience for us. So many things, like the shape of railwaymen's uniform caps, the appearance of telephone booths, and the format of notices were so different from our English equivalents and yet completely familiar, if not from the memory of 1936, then from films that had been made in Britain during the war. I found that I was still fluent in German and could follow any conversation in spite of the fact that I had not spoken or heard any German for twelve years. I found on this and on subsequent visits to Germany that, just as in England, regional variations in dialects and accents are now much less marked than they once were. This is the result not only of radio, television, and films, but also the consequence of the enormous number of Germans who had to change their homes after the war.

On this and on later visits to Germany I have always, initially, been very much impressed by the knowledge of music, of literature, and of art that people reveal in conversation. It was only after a considerable time that I realised that everyone was familiar with the same five symphonies and the same half-dozen operas and the same classic novels and could enumerate the same masterpieces of the same handful of painters. What seems to be much less common abroad than in England is the gifted amateur: the civil servant who writes sonnets, the surgeon who constructs violins, and the mechanic who paints in watercolours.

This has been a long digression from the tale of our journey, probably because the end of the tale was such a sad one. We did eventually reach the sanatorium in the Black Forest but, after we had been there for a week, it became obvious that my father's state was deteriorating. On the advice of a specialist, it was decided that he should return to England as soon as possible for a further operation, an operation that he did not survive. He was only sixty-three when he died. His life had been a hard one; he had to face poverty, war, revolution, unemployment during the Depression, political persecution, and emigration. He faced these vicissitudes with courage and cheerfulness, sustained by a very happy marriage to my mother. He was a loving, kind, and generous father, of whom I saw far too little; he always worked long hours and could take few holidays. I can only remember five family holidays between 1924 and 1950.

My father's great interest was engineering. All his life he regretted that financial problems had prevented him from staying at school and going on to acquire engineering qualifications. I think he was disappointed when I decided to study physics at Cambridge. He would have preferred me to take the path that was denied to him. He was fond of quoting the tag that a scientist's job is to investigate the world as it is, but an engineer's is to study a world that he has created himself.

He would have been glad to know that my research career consisted largely of the design of instruments and the development of new techniques. When I want to be modest in England, I say that I am not a real physicist, but more of an engineer: in France, I describe myself as not a real engineer but only a physicist.

Royal Institution, 1950–1956

Immediately after my return from Germany, I started my new job in London in the Davy-Faraday Laboratory of the Royal Institution, in Albemarle Street, London, W1. In retrospect, it seemed that I was entering into an age that now appears long past. The resident professorship at the RI, then filled by Professor EN da C Andrade was, and still is, in part a social position. The professor lived in a flat above the Institution and acted as host to members and visitors who attended the weekly Friday Evening Discourses. These lectures started on the stroke of 9 p.m. and lasted for exactly sixty minutes. Most of them were on topical scientific subjects, but they were interspersed with occasional literary or arts lectures. Lecturer and audience were in evening dress and, after the discourse, refreshments were served and one inspected the exhibits, in the library, of objects connected with the subject of the lecture.

In order to attract eminent scientists to the resident professorship, they required a laboratory and a scientific staff to pursue their own researches. A committee of managers, who were elected by the members of the RI, was nominally in charge of running it, sometimes in a tug-of-war with the resident professor. The latter was often referred to as the director, but he was 'director in the RI' and not 'of the RI'. In the eyes of the managers and some of the members, the staff of the laboratory were regarded as being, more or less, on a par with the director's domestic staff, although on Friday evenings most of us shed our lab coats for evening dress and attended the discourse.

Laboratory facilities and equipment depended on how much funding the director and other researchers could attract from government and private sources. It was usually easier to get some funding for research purposes than for keeping the white marble white and the red carpets red in the 'club' part of the building and this was one of the causes of friction between successive directors and committees of managers.

Conditions for the staff of about twenty were very pleasant. There was a staff restaurant with service by a waitress in a black dress and a frilly apron and, in the morning, the resident manageress came round the building taking orders for lunch.

The laboratory part of the building was served by a hydraulic lift that was operated by opening a valve by means of a rope which passed through the lift cage. The basement corridor was shared with Cartier, the jewellers, based next door in Albemarle Street. From time to time, one of their staff, accompanied by a security guard, would pass through carrying priceless jewellery on green baize-covered trays from their strong room to their shop basement.

I worked mostly in the basement laboratory, which housed the biggest X-ray tube in the world. This room had been used by previous directors, including Michael Faraday and Sir James Dewar, and much of their apparatus, now between fifty and one hundred years old, was still on shelves on the walls and in the vault which extended under Albemarle Street. It was in this laboratory that Dame Kathleen Lonsdale had carried out her celebrated X-ray investigation on the structure of ice crystals. Her paper on this work ends with the sentence, 'The work was carried out at room temperature, minus two degrees Celsius.' The room has since been turned into a Faraday museum and equipped with heating to protect the exhibits, among them Faraday's great electromagnet and Dewar's vacuum flasks

One was always conscious of the past at the RI. Some years later, I left a box of films on the bench of the instrument maker who worked in the room opposite the big laboratory. When I came to use the films a few days later, they were all heavily fogged. A portable Geiger counter that I brought in showed a highly radioactive area about five feet in diameter immediately under the instrument maker's feet. An anti-contamination team was brought in from the Harwell Atomic Energy Research Establishment, who took up the wooden flooring and the concrete below it to a depth of about six inches. While they were operating in plastic suits and breathing masks, the lab was visited by an old man who had worked there about fifty years before and who wanted to know what was going on. When he was told, he said: 'Oh, yes, I remember. Mme Curie gave a vial of radium chloride to Professor Dewar, who came down from his flat in the middle of the night to check whether it was true that radium glowed in the dark and the long sleeves of his dressing gown knocked the bottle on the floor.'

My first battles in the laboratory were with, or perhaps I should say against, the fifty kilowatt X-ray tube. Depending on one's point of view, it was either a wonderful example of 1930's electrical engineering or a fearful monster that had to be mastered by cunning and force. The two-foot diameter target of the brute was rotated by a ten horsepower electric motor through a long vacuum seal, consisting of many leather disks smeared with vacuum grease. When the motor was running, it emitted a high-pitched screech that left one deafened for half an hour after it was switched off. When one of the controlling relays or ammeters in the high-voltage enclosure got stuck, one had to lean over the safety fence and give the offending part a clout with a long piece of wood kept specially for that purpose. A run at full power was usually ended by the blowing of the 200-ampère fuses. The molten copper from the fuses had then to be removed from the fuse box with a chisel.

Unfortunately the electron focus, that is, the area from which the X-rays were emitted, was so large that when one was examining a small specimen, as we always wanted to, only a small fraction of the generated X-ray intensity reached the specimen. When I introduced X-ray sensitive Geiger counters to measure the X-ray intensity quantitatively, I was able to show that the monster produced fewer X-rays than a commercial X-ray tube that could be switched on and off as easily as an electric light bulb. But how could I, as the new boy in the laboratory, persuade the management that it would be best to scrap the pride and joy of the laboratory and buy a small commercial tube? Fortunately, at that time, the president of the Royal Institution was Lord Brabazon of Tara, former minister of aviation and holder of British pilot's licence number one. The Bristol Aircraft giant passenger plane, which was intended to dominate transatlantic traffic routes, was named the Brabazon. At about this time, it was decided that the plane was uneconomic and its construction was scrapped. In comparison, the scrapping of the X-ray tube was a small matter. I am not sure that I really believe that the two issues were connected, but at any rate, no objections were raised to my plans.

My next experimental achievements were more successful. I had the idea of replacing the Geiger counters, which had a limited intensity range, with another type of gas-filled counting tube named a proportional counter. To construct such a device required glass-blowing abilities beyond anything available to me. It had to be completely airtight and filled with a carefully metred mixture of gases. I constructed a demountable device, largely made from metal and sealed with rubber gaskets. By continuously flowing the appropriate gas mixture through the counter, I avoided the need for very high vacuum techniques, since small leaks round the gaskets and through the thin window through which the X-rays entered did not matter with a sufficiently high flow rate.

The building of the gas mixing and filling plant was easy as suitable pipelines, taps, gauges, tee-pieces as well as other junctions and pumps were in the RI store cupboards, left over from Dewar's gas liquefaction experiments. Adaptations of our 'flow counter' have since been widely used with extremely thin X-ray transparent entrance windows for the detection of very soft X-rays with a low penetrating power. In this work and in the construction of semi-automatic instruments for measuring the X-ray scattering from solutions and from powders of proteins, I was greatly assisted by Bill Coates, the future RI lectures assistant, who became well-known through his elaborate and ingenious lecture demonstrations, many of which were televised. Bill was a genius at picking up useful government surplus components for a few pence from the many shops in London's Soho, which specialised in such equipment. Our instruments were largely constructed from these sources.

With the help of our automated apparatus, my boss, Dennis Riley, and I were able to collect large volumes of data on many different biological materials. It was at that time by no means certain that Perutz and Kendrew in Cambridge, and other small teams of crystallographers in Oxford and elsewhere, would succeed in solving the detailed structure of proteins from measurements on crystallised material. We were hoping to derive more limited information, by comparing the conclusions from many related compounds, to arrive at useful results. In particular, we wanted to discover whether the helical structural feature proposed by Linus Pauling, in Pasadena, was present in many proteins. We published a considerable number of papers in the scientific literature, but our 'get-rich-quick' method and our conclusions have not stood the test of time and have been disproved by the much more labour-intensive crystallographic measurements, which, in the meantime, have also been automated, to some extent as a result of my own later work.

Life in London in the early 1950s was very pleasant. My mother had joined me and we had found a flat in Kensington Court, just behind the Milestone Hotel in Kensington High Street. We were on the third floor, up sixty-five steps with no lift. The front of the block was quite impressive but the back, to the north, had been damaged by a bomb and been rebuilt with a single thickness of bricks so that it was pretty cold. The only form of heating in the flat was a small coal-burning grate in the living room so we bought some electric fires. The water was heated by a gas geyser in the kitchen. But the rooms were large and not dwarfed by our big German furniture. We were ten minutes away from the Round Pond in Kensington Gardens. Living as we did reinforced the feeling, which working at the Royal Institution was also giving me, that time had stood still since Edwardian days. Kensington Court was illuminated by gas lamps, which were lit every evening by a man on a bicycle who, without dismounting, operated the tap inside each individual lamp by means of a long stick. The milk came in a horse-drawn cart, the milkman delivering every bottle to the appropriate floor, and the horse moved on to the next door when instructed by a click of his master's tongue. Later, when we lived in that flat with two small children, the same milkman told me that in the sixty blocks, with probably about five hundred flats, there were only four children in Kensington Court. I have always regretted that I never asked the milkman, who looked like a Spanish grandee, whether in real life John Buchan's Richard Hannay would have got away with impersonating the milkman at the beginning of *The Thirty-Nine Steps*. Surely the horse would not have moved on to the next house on a stranger's tongue clicking?

The original film version of this book with Robert Donat and Madeleine Carroll was an example of a book of average merit being turned into a first-class film. Other examples were Leslie Howard as Baroness Orczy's *The Scarlet Pimpernel* and, again, the first version of Anthony Hope's *Prisoner of Zenda*. As against that, great novels do not often make great films: I have never greatly appreciated any of the various attempts to make films of Jane Austen's novels or, to go from the sublime to the ridiculous, have I liked any film versions of P. G. Wodehouse's masterpieces. I have just re-read Tolkien's *Lord of the Rings* after an interval of many years and after having seen the films of the book. I have found that the films, excellent as they were, spoilt one of my favourite stories for me and removed much of the magic.

London being London, we, of course, knew very few of our neighbours. We could only afford to live at an address which Jim Hackforth-Jones in his best man's speech at our wedding was to describe as 'A good address to get married from,' because our rent was controlled. Today, few people other than oil sheiks can afford to live there. In those uncrowded days, before parking meters, I could usually park my car in front of our block of flats or in Albemarle Street, in front of the Royal Institution. In 1957, when I spent a sabbatical year at the University of Wisconsin in Madison, I explained my clumsiness at backing into a parking slot by explaining that in London one could usually drive in forwards into any desired place at the kerbside. By the time I came back, in 1958, the situation had changed. But it was more comfortable to go to the RI by number nine bus, ten minutes for two and a half old pence (one new penny) or on a fine day to walk the two miles through Kensington Gardens, Hyde Park and Green Park. At lunchtime, it was only a few minutes walk to the Royal Academy and even not too far to the National Gallery. In the evening, in addition to the Friday evening discourses at the RI, I often went to the theatre or to the National Film Theatre. The redevelopment of the South Bank was a symbol of the end of post-war austerity and the 1951 Festival of Britain and the 'Britain Can

Make It' exhibition contributed to the general optimism about the economic future, optimism that received severe knocks with the fatigue failures of the Comet, the pride of the British aircraft industry.

The early 1950s also saw the appearance all over the West End of espresso bars, so that for the first time there was an alternative to going to a pub after a play or a film.

I have vivid recollections of the 1952 coronation procession, in pouring rain, and of the tented camps for colonial troops which arose in Kensington Gardens.

Another memory of that period is that of the last great 'pea souper fog' in 1952, when road traffic in London was virtually halted, when the guards of tube trains could not see along the length of the platform whether passengers were boarding the train, and when theatres were open but put out warning notices that the stage was visible only from the front rows of the stalls. The gathering places in London for dwellers in furnished flats were the laundrettes, the do-it-yourself laundries with coin-operated washing machines. For weeks after the great fog they were overcrowded with people washing the soot and grime out of their linen and curtains.

It was very exciting being able to travel abroad again and I derived great pleasure from a mini Grand Tour in 1952. I spent a few days in Holland, where I stayed in Rotterdam with my Emmanuel friend Tony Fisher who, after demobilisation and a period as a management trainee, was working in the Dutch office of Unilever. I also met some of my Dutch and Belgian relatives for the first and, in some cases, the last time. There was a somewhat difficult reunion conducted in a mixture of English, German, French and Dutch.

I was particularly impressed by Rotterdam, where the central area had been flattened by German bombs in 1940 and rebuilding was in full swing. Rotterdam harbour was like an anthill with enormous activity going on in transhipping cargo from ocean-going ships to Rhine barges. I passed through Rotterdam again some thirty years later, when the total annual cargo handled had more than doubled, but the harbour, in contrast, seemed quiet and serene. The development of container traffic and the automation of the loading facilities were enormously more efficient. I am reminded here of an amiable Dutchman whom I met some years later at a snow-bar after a ski-run down to Courchevel. He described himself as 'the biggest sucker in Rotterdam', by which he meant that he owned the largest hydraulic grain elevator in the harbour.

One of the pleasures of travelling on the Continent in the 1950s was the popularity of the British. In Scandinavia and in the Netherlands everyone seemed to be keen to practise or to show off their English. When I came out of the railway station in Rotterdam, studying a tourist map, a pleasant man in a dog collar asked me whether he could help me. When I told him my destination, he said that he was going in the same direction and would show me the way.

'I know that everyone in Holland speaks perfect English,' I said to him, 'but surely you are just too good to be true; surely you are English!'

'Certainly not,' was the reply, 'I am the Minister of the Scots Kirk in Rotterdam! And I might add that I am probably the only man in Rotterdam who resents being taken for an Englishman!'

My friend Jack Dunitz also has a Dutch story to tell. He was walking in Holland with a Dutch friend when a large German Mercedes stopped and the driver, in very poor English, asked the way to a certain hotel. Jack asked his friend why the German had spoken English when practically everyone in Holland spoke even better German?

'If he had spoken German,' he replied, 'I would have pretended not to understand him.'

'But when he uses English you answer him?'

'Yes, but I sent him in the wrong direction!'

From Holland, I went by train to Hamburg to see the family's lawyer and then by ferry to Fyn and to Zealand, where I spent several days in Copenhagen, admiring the impeccable Danish taste in the modern shops as well as visiting Hamlet's mediaeval castle of Elsinore. But even the Tivoli Gardens in Copenhagen seemed to me to be gay and amusing while avoiding the tawdriness and tastelessness of fairgrounds elsewhere. From

Copenhagen's Kastrup Airport, where the airline staff travelled around on scooters, to Stockholm (more museums and more attractive modern interior and exterior architecture) and thence to Oslo by train. I had just settled into my seat when an elegant blonde stopped by my table. I was about to jump to my feet and introduce myself when the Nordic goddess produced a feather duster and then refilled my water carafe.

On a visit to Sweden a few summers later, I asked a Swedish friend why it was that this rich and beautiful country, where all the inhabitants looked healthy and well-dressed, had the highest suicide rate and produced the gloomiest literature and the most depressing films.

'Come back in six months time,' he answered, 'and you will understand.'

In fact, when I visited Oslo once in early December, I found it very depressing to see a blood-red sun stagger barely above the horizon just before noon and disappear again almost at once. However, on this trip, I found Oslo very attractive and paid my respects to Thorwaldsen's statues and to Heyerdahl's *Kon-tiki* raft. By this time, I had had enough of tramping through city streets and museum galleries and was glad to follow the itinerary suggested to me by a Norwegian friend in London. This was to walk westwards through Jotunheimen and to stay in a series of delightful tourist hostels in the mountains.

At first, I found the going tough as each day I marched between six and eight hours across rough and steep paths. In some of the more luxurious huts, one could get one's reward in a sauna at the end of the day. Later in life, I did quite a lot of strenuous walking in the English Lake District, in Wales, and in the Alps, with and without children, and I have always regretted that I left a repeat of this wonderful Norwegian walking tour until I was no longer capable of it.

I finished my holiday in Bergen, where I retrieved my luggage and spent the last night before catching the Newcastle ferry in the only scruffy bed and breakfast lodging I have ever encountered in Scandinavia. Here I had to share a double bed with an unsympathetic elderly man whose breakfast in the morning consisted of two bottles of beer and a wicked-smelling cigar. I fled without witnessing his ablutions and ended my sightseeing in this attractive city with lunch in the elegant restaurant on the Floyelen at the top of a cliff overlooking the harbour. While I was enjoying a beer, looking down on the ferry I was to board that evening, I was surprised to be greeted with a broad smile by the smart headwaiter who wanted to know whether I would again be sharing his bed that night at Fru Rasmussen's.

I should perhaps add that when I next visited Bergen over forty years later with Valerie, at the start of a Norwegian Cruise up the coast to the North Cape, the view from the Floyelen was every bit as fine as I remembered, but the elegance of the restaurant had much decayed, either in my appreciation or in fact. Perhaps I was making comparisons with the hotel where we were staying, instead of with Fru Rasmussen's B&B.

In retrospect, I must have been pretty idle in the 1950s. I had three skiing holidays in Austria and in Norway. Having sailed a lot on the Norfolk Broads, I was keen to extend my experience to sea-going sailing yachts. I joined the Little Ship Club and went to lectures on seamanship and coastal navigation. There were plenty of boats available for charter on the south coast, but their condition at times was not exactly perfect. In time, I assembled a kit to make sailing a little easier and safer. This included a plentiful supply of duct tape for under-way repairs, a number of shock cords for fixing halyards to the mast and to the shrouds to give one peace at night, and a few pieces of chamois leather and a funnel for filtering the petrol after washing out the tank: the tank was often corroded and, to prevent sudden stopping of the engine, it was advisable to dismantle the petrol tank and to wash it out several times after banging its outside to dislodge flakes of rust.

My diciest sailing trip was one on which I went with my Emmanuel friend, Graham Lee, when we flew out to Norway to join two undergraduates, ex-RNVR sub lieutenants, whom the owner had engaged to sail his forty-ton Colin Archer ex-pilot ketch to England after a re-fit in a Norwegian boatyard for a proposed cruise round the world while he, the owner, was earning enough money by skippering other people's boats in the Mediterranean.

When Graham and I arrived in Norway, we found that money had run out and the yard had stopped work on the ketch, with a lot of work left undone. The four of us set to work in order to make things a little more shipshape before the equinoctual gales set in. Even so, the anchor winch had not been rigged and the compressor for the hydraulic starter for the diesel engine was not working when we set off. Without these two vital components, we decided to forgo any trials or shakedown practice sails along the Norwegian coast but to go straight away across the North Sea to Harwich. After twenty-four hours in a flat calm, the Norwegian coast had just disappeared when it started to blow.

In a force eight gale the genoa, our only fair-weather sail, blew out, whereupon we discovered that there was no sailmaker's kit on board. With considerable effort, and with the help of a rusty file, I succeeded in making a needle out of a sardine tin key. It continued to blow very hard and we were forced to heave to under mizzen and repaired genoa, feeling fairly miserable and being tossed about so much that cooking a hot meal was impossible. We existed on a bowl of cornflakes with condensed milk and a tin of fifty duty-free cigarettes a day. (It took me thirty years to break myself of the habit of smoking cigarettes.)

On the sixth morning, we sighted a low-lying coast to lee-ward. It was still blowing a westerly gale and we did not succeed in starting the diesel engine to counter our drift towards the easterly shore. We hoisted a bucket to the crosstrees as a distress signal and we were seen by a low-flying SAS Dakota, which radioed a nearby trawler who arrived in the nick of time to tow us off. Passing a wire hawser was very difficult. At one moment we were at the same height as the trawler's mast top; the next, the trawler's mast top was level with us. The hawser parted twice until we shackled on a long length of our anchor cable. We were towed due north most of the day and then, at midnight, we turned east, leaving us completely puzzled as to where we were. We could not understand the shouted instructions from the trawler and this was in the days before global position indicators.

At daybreak, we again turned south and some hours later we entered a harbour on our starboard side. It was then that we realised that we had been picked up off the Jutland coast near the

German-Danish frontier and had been towed through the Skagerak into the Baltic and were now lying in the harbour of Frederikshaven, near the north-eastern tip of Jutland.

Our companions' time was their own and so they stayed in Denmark and dealt with the salvage claim put in by the Danish fishermen. The claim was surprisingly low and was eventually settled for £200, which was raised by selling the motor lifeboat that we had carried upside-down on deck. It was too large for the ketch and had been acquired by the owner for a later sale. The wind resistance offered by this large object probably accounted for our being blown to leeward instead of making slow progress at about forty-five degrees to the wind direction as a well-behaved yacht should when hove-to.

Graham and I had to get back to our jobs as quickly as possible and succeeded in getting a passage that same day on a tramp steamer from nearby Aalborg to Newcastle. It was still so rough in the North Sea that our ship hove-to for twelve hours. Graham and I had by now got our sea legs and also colossal appetites. The sight of the two of us demolishing the breakfast laid out for six passengers was too much for the stewardess, who retired to her bunk and left us a free run of the galley.

Undeterred by these adventures, I chartered a yacht in Copenhagen the next summer, advertised on the Little Ship Club notice board and much cheaper than anything available in Britain. My crew was a South African couple, both complete novices at sailing and, perhaps because of that, undeterred by my account of my adventures the previous year. Shortly before our departure, they phoned me to come round for drinks and to meet someone who was also about to sail in Danish waters. He turned out to be a straight-laced ex-RN commander, who had been engaged by the owner of a forty ton Colin Archer ketch, which some bloody fools had failed to sail home from Norway and had left in Denmark for him to bring home. Of course, I had to confess that I was one of the bloody fools and was put through a most uncomfortable cross-examination on why we had not done this or the other. I think that what I told him persuaded him that he needed a strong crew, a working radio and better arrangements for preparing hot meals.

After a very successful holiday in Denmark, during which we sailed round Zealand, I met the somewhat chastened ex-naval officer in London in the autumn. He had sailed through the Limfjord and had got stuck on the mud at its western end. While the ketch was being towed off by a powerful tug, it had sprung a leak and he had then made for Aberdeen with one member of his strong crew always at the bilge pump. In Scotland, his crew left him and he had recruited a new crew on the quayside with whom he got to Lowestoft, whence he went up the river Waveney to Beccles. He left the ketch up a creek and I saw her there a couple of years later, when she looked as though no wave would ever be high enough to make her rock to the slightest extent.

My friend and sailing companion, Jim Hackforth-Jones, and his wife, Mary, had produced two children, Mark and Toria, in quick succession and as a result they were not readily available to crew for Jim's parents, Gilbert and Margaret. So I came to do quite a lot of sailing with them on their yacht which Gilbert, as a retired naval commander, always kept in a pristine condition. He insisted that the shrouds should be set up in such a way that, when twanged, they went 'Ping' and not 'Pong', whereas on the charter yachts to which I was accustomed, they went 'woodda-woodda'.

Gilbert, after retiring from the navy, had become a professional writer of sea stories and, as such, he had persuaded the inspector of taxes that keeping his own yacht was a legitimate business expense. He had written a very successful series of radio plays about the sailing adventures of the Green family, called 'The Green Sailors', for the BBC's children's hour. He once took me along to the studio at Langham Place for the recording of an episode. I was amused to see that Norman Shepherd, who played the part of the salt-encrusted deep-sea sailor uncle of the child heroes and who had a voice which would have been clearly audible while rounding Cape Horn in a gale, was in fact a short, tubby man of a decidedly un-nautical appearance. Like many actors with wonderful voices, he was not really suited for television plays and acted only in radio. I once sailed with Gilbert and Margaret on a beautiful summer's day in a light breeze when Norman was the other guest. He was given the wheel for half an hour and told to steer straight down the middle of the Solent. At the end of his trick, he handed the wheel back to Gilbert with the words, 'I trust, commander, that I have steered a satisfactory course.'

I had the opportunity of admiring Gilbert's professional skill as a writer. He was writing a novel, published under the title *One Man's War,* in which his hero was landed by helicopter on the deck of an enemy cruiser off the Norwegian coast in order to wreck the German warship. Gilbert asked me whether I could translate naval orders from English into German and when I replied that I would not be able, in every case, to be completely certain of the German, he asked me to mark my translated phrases 'one' (when I was sure of the correctness), 'two' (when I was probably right), and 'three' (when I was quite uncertain). In the book, number one phrases were used as they stood, number two were put into the mouths of Germans and described as 'or that was what it sounded like', and number three were spoken by the English hero with the comment, 'he mumbled and hoped that he had got it right'. In the book it all seems completely natural.

In the laboratory I probably did not work as hard as today's postdocs are working, or say they are working, in the present competitive atmosphere. However, I did get quite a lot of work done that led to a reasonable number of publications in the scientific literature. I learnt some lessons on how to get on in science from my boss, but some of his lessons were best ignored. Dennis wrote scientific papers well, if not very concisely. When he had finished a ten-page paper, he would compose an extra four pages, of no very great relevance to the rest of the paper, and insert these pages somewhere in the middle of his manuscript. When he received the inevitable referee's request that the paper be somewhat shortened, he would offer, 'as a concession to the referee's advice, to remove pages four to seven'.

He had spent a period as scientific attaché at Duff Cooper's British embassy in Paris and, as a result, received many French visitors at the Royal Institution. In those days, English had not yet become the universal scientific language and, if you wanted to discuss something with a French or a German, it was highly advisable to do it in their language. This was still true at the first international conference of crystallography that I attended in Paris in 1954. But scientists one generation older than I had often spent post-doctoral years in continental Europe in the 1920s and 1930s and consequently were fluent in German, French, and even Danish or Dutch. After about 1950, any scientist who was, or who wanted to be, anyone tried to organise a visit to the United States, and American English became the language of science.

I have mentioned above that the possibility of friction arose at the Royal Institution as a result of the conflicting requirements of the research laboratory and of the needs for other facilities demanded by the body of members of the Royal Institution, many of whom were primarily interested in the social functions. In 1952 there was a full conflagration, which ended in a vote of no confidence in the director, Professor Andrade. After a sad wrangle, Andrade was forced to resign and the laboratory was supervised by Mr Ryde of the GEC until a new director could be appointed.

Dennis Riley had been hoping to be asked to step into the directorship but his hopes were in vain, partly because he had been too obviously in the anti-Andrade camp to find much favour in the reconciliation era. One of Dennis's last activities was to give a Friday Evening Discourse; he had the temerity to make his title *The Chemistry of an Egg*, in imitation of one of the most famous lectures given by Michael Faraday, on *The Chemistry of a Candle*. Eggs at that time were still rationed, but the Egg Marketing Board were very helpful in providing a good supply of particularly large and beautiful eggs. Dennis started his lecture with the words 'A simple egg, yet, within its fragile shell, it hides all the secrets of life itself.' He then proceeded to break an egg into a bowl of oil. Traditionally, the lecturer at the RI is locked into a small room for five minutes before the lecture, where he is provided with a generous glass of whiskey to settle his nerves. The tradition dates back to Professor Wheatstone, inventor of the Wheatstone Bridge, who escaped in fear down Albemarle Street just before the start of his discourse. I could see the look of suspicion that Dennis cast at the egg in the bowl. This turned to sheer panic when the second extra large egg turned out, like the first one, to be double yolked. The look of relief on his face when he caught some whispers from the audience, 'Look: double yolked eggs,' was altogether beautiful to behold.

I now feel more charitable towards Dennis. Ten years later, I was asked to deliver a discourse at the RI. Familiar as I was, and irreverent as I had become after twelve years there, I found it an altogether terrifying experience. To stand at the lectern and to look at the serried ranks of boiled shirts and evening dresses in the amphitheatre is somehow a greater strain than any other lecturing I have done, at home or abroad.

Andrade was keen that as many of the laboratory staff as possible should leave after his departure. He arranged for me to go and see Professor John Randall and Maurice Wilkins at King's College London. As I was washing my hands before lunch, Maurice, whom I knew fairly well, turned to me and said: 'You cannot possibly want to work in the same place as that woman,' (meaning Rosalind Franklin, whom I also knew quite well). Their mutual antagonism has since been described in scurrilous detail. I could sense that there was something a little unhealthy in the atmosphere at King's and did not pursue the possibility of a job there.

Fortunately, at about this time Sir Lawrence Bragg resigned from the Cavendish professorship at Cambridge and accepted the job of Resident Professor and Director of the laboratory at the Royal Institution. He did so out of loyalty to the RI, where his father had been director for many years. He was persuaded by the well-wishers of the RI that he was the only eminent scientist with sufficient standing to heal the wounds left by the 'troubles'. The appointment was a very happy one for the institution. Bragg was a brilliant populariser of science; he gave a new purpose to the institution with lecture series to schoolchildren, schoolteachers, and civil servants. Some of these lectures were televised from the RI lecture theatre and had a far greater impact than mere studio productions. Without Bragg's influence and enthusiasm, and without his innovations, the existing traditional Friday evening discourses and the Christmas lectures, 'adapted for a juvenile auditory', would probably have been regarded as elitist and anachronistic and in the end they would have lapsed.

In addition, Bragg built up a school of protein crystallography.

He attempted to attract Max Perutz and John Kendrew from Cambridge to London and, when neither of them could move, he appointed them Readers in Crystallography at the RI. John Kendrew, in particular, took his office very seriously and visited London very regularly to guide the fledgling group and to encourage collaboration with what was then the MRC Unit of Molecular Biology and which developed into the MRC Laboratory of Molecular Biology. I was the first one to be recruited into the new group and was appointed to the Dewar Research Fellowship. I was followed by Helen Scouloudi from Birkbeck College, David Green from Cambridge, Tony North from King's College London, and, most importantly, David Phillips, who had been working in Ottawa.

While I was still engaged in writing up for publication the rest of the work that I had been doing with Riley, I undertook the job of supervising the construction and installation of two new X-ray tubes designed by Tony Broad in Cambridge, so that X-ray crystallographic studies by photographic methods could be started by the others as soon as possible. I also got the workshop to manufacture a three-circle X-ray diffractometer, which I equipped with one of my proportional X-ray detectors. (By international agreement it had been decided to call these instruments 'diffractometers' when their main function was to record diffraction patterns, reserving the term 'spectrometer' for instruments used for measuring X-ray wavelengths.) On the diffractometer, the specimen could be orientated by rotations about three axes to pick up each of the thousands of X-ray spectra, or 'reflections', in turn. The settings of the axes had to be worked out on a digital computer and, when David Phillips joined in this work, we found it very inconvenient to have the tables of these settings computed on the Cambridge electronic computer, EDSAC. At this time, computers were still very rare and expensive and we saw little prospect of getting access to one in London. Accordingly, we worked out an analogue method, in which we rotated transparent protractors over a scale drawing of the crystal lattice and read off-the-shaft settings on the angle scales. This worked quite well but it was still very laborious.

David remarked to me one Friday what a pity it was that the

rotations of the protractors could not be linked directly to those of the crystal shafts and thus automate the diffractometer. I was spending the following weekend with the Hackforth-Jones family. Borrowing Mark's Meccano set, I tried out possible linkages for such an automatic instrument. Designing and prototyping took another two years, complicated by the fact that much of the design consultation had to be done by trans-Atlantic airmail letters, as I had undertaken to spend a sabbatical year in the department of Bill Beeman at the University of Wisconsin in Madison during 1957. However, soon after my return in the spring of 1958, we were able to exhibit a working prototype instrument at the annual Physical Society exhibition. We called our machine 'The Linear Diffractometer'. It was the first automatic diffractometer and it was manufactured under licence by Hilger and Watts Ltd, who sold about one hundred of these machines worldwide.

By the time the commercial linear diffractometer had been brought to market, it was already out of date: the development of electronic digital computers had been much faster than any of us had expected and it soon became clear that the way ahead lay with general purpose digital computers, which could communicate with the external machines by means of punched paper tapes and punched cards, as was becoming the practice with automatic machine tools, such as lathes and milling machines. For many years, this office equipment remained the weak link in laboratory automation, in spite of its very wide use in automated offices. The machines were just not sufficiently robust for continuous unattended operation over many hours. The reliability problems were only generally overcome around 1970 by direct digital data transfer between scientific instruments and computers. The computers of the 1950s filled a small room, but they were rapidly becoming smaller and more suitable for building into data collecting instruments. The computers of the late 1960s were the size of a suitcase while the computers built into today's scientific instruments could be put into a matchbox.

In the 1950s, the danger to health from exposure to X-rays was at last being taken seriously. Prior to that period, risks were taken that now seem quite intolerable. One of the worst abuses was the installation of X-ray tubes in every shoe shop, so that one could check the fit of a pair of shoes by observing the shadow of one's feet inside the shoes on a fluorescent screen. The devices were used by adults and children alike. A choosy shopper who tried on several pairs would receive a dangerous overdose. Early X-ray crystallographers were also far from careful in the laboratory and burnt fingers and X-ray induced cataracts were not uncommon. By the time I was a research student, sensible precautions were being taken and all workers who risked being exposed to X-rays carried dose meters and had regular blood counts. I can think of no serious accident due to overexposure to X-rays among X-ray crystallographers anywhere in the world among my contemporaries.

At one point in 1955, my blood count was found to be rather low and I was advised to stay away from the laboratory for four weeks. (It was decided later that the lowered count had probably been due to a bout of flu, so the long skiing holiday which I took, and which changed my life, was probably unnecessary.) I spent the first half of February in Obergurgl, where I greatly improved my skiing and got very fit, spending all daylight hours on skis. After two weeks, I moved on to Lech, where the company was rather more interesting. I was particularly attracted to a tall, good-looking girl called Valerie. At the first breakfast, I was asked to translate the notices pinned up in every room in the hotel which read '*Kissen und Decken dürfen nicht aus den Zimmern auf die Terrasse genommen werden*,' which I rendered 'Kissing and necking is not allowed in the rooms but only on the terrace.' This was greeted with surprise by all the party but by explosive laughter from Valerie, whose languages were French and Spanish, but not German. Reader: I married her three years later.

I was sufficiently interested in Valerie to take her out every two to three weeks after our return to London; always to a restaurant and never the theatre or cinema. It seemed such a waste of the company of an interesting conversationalist to spend our time together sitting in silence in the dark. Taking a young woman to a restaurant had its problems, also. It always worried my mean heart to see a lady-like half of a delicious Soho meal left on my companion's plate while I was still hungry. There was no such problem with Valerie when we had a Chinese meal; she had spent some of her early childhood in Shanghai, where her father was stationed in the RAMC, and she had taken a strong liking to Chinese food. Valerie told me later that she puzzled over what I did in the evenings in the intervals between seeing her. Among her acquaintances it was very unusual for a young man to be working most evenings at his job.

In the summer of 1956, I had to attend a crystallographic meeting in Madrid and, together with my colleagues, David Green and Helen Scouloudi, decided to hire a car in Ostende and to drive to Madrid via Carcassone, Barcelona, Valencia, and Andalusia, arriving in Granada and Seville during Holy Week. As none of us knew any Spanish apart from the all-important phrase '*sin ajo*' (without garlic), I tried in vain to persuade Valerie to come with us as an interpreter. It never occurred to me to explain to her that I was not proposing a *partie à deux* or *à deux couples* and so, as a well brought up young lady, Valerie had to refuse.

The trip was not a wild success. It turned out that David had never driven after dark before and that Helen could not drive at all and could not read a map. In the south, it poured with rain without cease and the gorgeous uniforms and the saints' images in the holy week processions were drenched. Besides, I found Franco's Spain unappealing. The omnipresent fascist slogans everywhere reminded me too much of Nazi Germany. Spain seemed to be full of organised groups of young Germans, who were guests of the Falange and who were obviously in search of Nazi *Paradise Lost*. The masses of pictures in the art galleries by Hieronymous Bosch, El Greco, and Goya seemed to indicate a taste very different from that in Italy, let alone that in northern Europe. After our conference, I felt we were practically home when we crossed into France, not far from San Sebastian, and could once again communicate with people around us.

Valerie later told me of her own experiences in Spain. She had made several exchange visits with a very kind and hospitable Spanish family, having stayed both in their Madrid home and in their holiday house in the seaside village of Benidorm. The latter was then a minute fishing village and Valerie's host, who was a civil engineer, was organising the water supply, which was to make possible the expansion of the village into a city of skyscrapers. It is now one of the sanctuaries of binge drinkers from all over northern Europe. Valerie also found the customs of Spain alien, especially as regarded the position of women. No one regretted the absence of women's right to vote. A young woman could not eat alone in a restaurant, or even go into the corner shop without being escorted by a man or a boy. Valerie and her sister Stefanie kept in touch with a son of their Spanish host, later, like his father, Professor of Engineering at Madrid University, who married a left wing Catalan journalist. He once told Valerie that, having got to know her and Stefanie, he could never have married into the Madrileno circles in which he had been brought up.

Spain, of course, has changed enormously in the last fifty years, as indeed has England. Only the other day, I was told by an American scientist who had last spent a period in my laboratory over twenty years ago that he found English speech, mores, clothes, and food unrecognisable from those he had known on his last visit.

Equally, the America that I saw during my sabbatical year in 1957 was probably closer to the USA where my father worked in 1908 than to the country it is today.

In the 1950s, one had not arrived in science until one had spent a period in the USA. My invitation to spend a year working with Bill Beeman in Madison had resulted from the time which John Anderegg from Bill's group had spent with Dennis and me at the Royal Institution. The Madison scientists were best known for their studies of solutions of proteins and other biological materials by X-ray scattering methods. The invitation came at a good time for me when I was trying to decide whether to go on with the sort of X-ray scattering studies on which I had been engaged or to concentrate on instrument development for single crystal structure determinations of proteins in collaboration with Max Perutz's team in Cambridge, which Sir Lawrence Bragg was introducing at the RI. Although I enjoyed my time in Madison very much, I found that, at the end of it, I dropped naturally into the design of single crystal instrumentation. The work I did in this field in collaboration, at first, with David Phillips and later with colleagues in Cambridge, helped greatly to accelerate X-ray data collection from protein crystals and thus the solution of the structures of the proteins myoglobin and haemoglobin, and many others.

United States, 1957–1958

On Boxing Day of 1956, I set off for my year in the USA, travelling tourist class on *RMS Ryndam* of the Holland-America line. At £56, one way, a sea crossing of the Atlantic was then still the most common and cheapest way of getting to the States, especially for someone with a lot of luggage. The trip was a very luxurious one, in spite of appalling weather which extended it to eleven days. One was woken up by the bath steward who had run one's bath, had an enormous breakfast at 9 a.m., morning coffee at 10.30 a.m., a five course lunch at 1.30 p.m., tea and biscuits at 4 p.m., and a six-course dinner at 7.30 p.m. Sandwiches and soup were available at 11 p.m., after the evening dance or concert. I shared a cabin with Bill Gallup, a middle-aged Texan, who was creeping home after half a lifetime of bumming around the world, having sold his house a week before oil was struck in his back-yard. He was my first introduction to the forms that the political thinking of ordinary Americans can take: he professed himself a liberal, yet asked me whether it was possible to sterilise young black boys without their knowledge by standing them under an X-ray tube. He was just hoping that his brother was sending him $300 to New York so that he would be able to buy a used car and drive home to Texas.

I can still remember the magic of steaming past the floodlit Statue of Liberty to dock under the towering cliffs of skyscrapers with their many shining windows. But I can also remember the rudeness and unpleasantness of the US Customs and Immigration when we were disembarked in the middle of the night. Together with Bill Gallup and some of my other shipboard acquaintances, we were bussed to the Times Square Hotel, then one of the cheapest hotels in Manhattan, during the small hours of the morning.

The next day, I visited Brooklyn Polytechnic, where I had been invited to give a talk. The unreality of transatlantic travel was brought home to me when I met Francis Crick and John Kendrew there. They had left Cambridge on the previous day and travelled by air, while I had taken twelve days over the journey.

I spent four days visiting friends and sightseeing in New York. My impressions were probably the same as those of any other European visitor at that time, but it may be worth quoting prices which I reported in my first letter home: breakfast in the hotel coffee shop, $1.10 (£0.40), and a steak in the cheapest restaurant $1.25, (£0.45). On my last evening in the hotel, I ran into Bill Gallup; after beating about the bush a little, he asked me how much money I would have on me when I arrived in Madison. Expecting a touch, I named a figure slightly on the low side, whereupon Bill said: 'That is not a lot for a young man in a strange country. Here, let me loan you $200, and if you cannot pay me back it's no great tragedy.' I had great difficulty in getting him to put his wallet back in his pocket.

We checked out at the same time the next morning. Bill asked the hall porter the way to the part of New York with the most used car dealers. A bystander offered to sell Bill his own car on the spot for $600. Another bystander in the meantime had phoned a dealer on Long Island and came back with a list of offers. Eventually he drove Bill there in his car; he was getting a commission of fifteen percent on the deal. A month later, I received a postcard in Madison from Bill. It had a photograph of a Texan longhorn steer with the caption, 'I just love Texas'. Bill wrote: 'I am now the roughest and toughest debt collector in the whole of Texas.'

I left New York by train, travelling day coach to save money, and took sixteen hours to Chicago, where I caught another train to Madison. Here the temperature was minus four degrees Fahrenheit (-20 degrees C). It took me quite a while to accustom myself to the fact that the sun high in a bright blue sky did not mean warm weather. During heavy frosts, one planned walks across the campus to lead through intervening buildings so as not to freeze on the way. After a snowfall, the ground presented a strange appearance. It was crossed by a grid of dark lines between the faculty buildings, the traces of the hot water pipes from the central heating plant that served the entire campus.

I was accommodated very conveniently in the Faculty Club, which was within a few minutes' walk from the university union, with its restaurants, coffee shops and bars, and also from the university library, the physics department and most shops. I had a simple but adequate room on the second floor of the Faculty Club. There were notices informing residents that it was against the custom to entertain ladies above the first floor. I wondered for a while who were the trusties on the lower floors who were considered safe for female company, until I discovered that, in American houses, the first floor is the ground floor, which here housed the reading and television rooms and the restaurant, which I rarely used.

The centre of Madison seemed very familiar and this was because it was so like the scenery of any American film set in small-town USA. The same was true of the campus, as it had been of the train and of parts of New York. I continued to feel for some time that soon the credit titles would come up and I would go outside and catch a number nine bus to Kensington and home.

My colleagues in the physics department, and indeed everyone I met in Madison, and elsewhere in the States, were incredibly hospitable and kind. At the first meeting, people went to great trouble to give me advice, to help with shopping and with negotiations with the bank, and with the university administration. I never lacked company at meal times and always had offers of lifts by car when I wanted to go somewhere. Yet I was not very happy during my first couple of months in Madison and felt rather homesick. This was partly the result of the very severe winter weather. I have often been aware of the basic hostility of the environment in large areas of the United States: too cold in winter and too hot and humid in summer. You feel that the malevolent weather is out to get you if the central heating furnace or the air-conditioning break down. And if the weather does not get you, there are snakes, bears, and skunks, not to mention delights like poison ivy. I had never properly appreciated the tameness of conditions in England until I had experienced the United States.

Another problem for me as a single man in the Middle West was the tedium of the almost exclusively male society. Many of my colleagues happened to be unmarried, but the married ones tended to leave their wives at home with the children and come out for a meal or a few beers with the boys only. At parties the men congregated at one end of the room and the women at the other end and it seemed that it was not done for an unattached male to cross the boundary. I was once invited to be the fourth in a mixed party at a dance. When the other couple got up to dance and I said: 'Shall we dance?' I was told by my blind date: 'Maybe in England you dance when you say "Dance". Here we dance when I say "Dance".' When she then said 'Dance' I was told that I danced like her pop. When the weather got warmer and the student population spent much of their time on the grass of the campus, it was obvious that initiatives were mostly taken by the girls

One of the mysteries of university life that I never solved was the following: on a given day all the co-eds (woman students), were clad in Bermuda shorts in various shades of luridness, the next day they all appeared in bobby socks, and, after a few days, there was another concerted change. Who gave the command and how it was passed on all over the campus remained unanswered questions.

Living so far from any foreign country, many Americans had little interest in what went on overseas. The automatic assumption was that, when there were differences in customs or institutions, the foreign ones must be inferior. I sympathised with an English expatriate who told me that she would have liked America better if she had ever been asked how she liked the country, instead of always: 'How do you like our wonderful country?' Having seen Paradise, surely the foreign visitor would never want to go home!

The differences between an English university, especially Oxford or Cambridge, and a mid-western state university were enormous. Since my time in Wisconsin, we have moved much closer to American practice in student selection and in the subjects studied, but there still remain big differences in the outlook of faculty members. Cambridge undergraduates of my generation were encouraged to feel that they were very privileged to be in the company of the great ones and had to be thankful for such crumbs of knowledge and wisdom as dropped from the high tables of their superiors. Many academics considered that teaching students interfered with their primary occupations in scholarship and research. In contrast, American professors are seen, and see themselves, as paid educators who take their teaching duties very seriously. I must have let my astonishment show when a physics professor, with whom I had been chatting, promised to see what he could do for him when asked rather brusquely by a student: 'Say, professor, I need to know some statistics for my research work; can you lay on a course?' I told my friend that an English professor would, at most, have given the student a list of suitable textbooks.

Most visitors from overseas had similar difficulties in acclimatising to American ways and felt that they had more in common with one another than with their hosts. But the ones who were least at home were not the genuine foreigners but the exiles from the East or West Coast and, especially, from the Ivy League universities. It was told of an eminent historian that, after thirty-five years in Wisconsin and one year from his retirement, he still looked eagerly into his letterbox every morning to see whether the summons back to his *alma mater* had arrived.

I derived much pleasure from the company of Jacques Blamont, a French physicist of about my age, who also stayed at the Faculty Club and with whom I often had breakfast in the union. As a typical Parisian intellectual, he did not like America very much and was rather suspicious of American scientists, whom he regarded as dangerous rivals. He was happy to discover that, 'They are no better than we are, there are just so many more of them'. He did not take to American food, which was 'just like American women, beautifully packaged, but completely without taste'. One morning he was uncharacteristically cheerful, 'Yesterday I went to a party and there were two women who were lesbians; I was so happy to find something so normal in Madison, Wisconsin'.

Just as the commitment of physics professors to their teaching seemed to me to be different from that of the majority of their opposite numbers in England, so did I also feel that the attitude to their research was different. For one thing, the Americans seemed less wrapped up in their own narrow speciality. Many people went to most of the colloquia and seminars given by visiting speakers, covering the whole range of physics, from nuclear physics and biophysics to solid state physics. Perhaps this was natural when performance at a seminar was so often the means of selecting a future faculty member and when any member of staff could be required at some time to give a course of undergraduate lectures on any branch of physics. In some ways the research was done less efficiently than at home, partly because of the priority given to teaching and partly because there were few full-time technicians, research support being provided by part-time undergraduate laboratory assistants and data takers. The time-tables of these students were, of course, dictated by lectures and preparations for examinations.

In American university laboratories it has always been customary for any individual researcher or group of research scientists to write a separate grant application. The resulting funds, if any, go to the applicant and there may be large differences in how well funded different members of the same department are. Compared with British laboratories, especially with research council laboratories, there are fewer central or shared facilities. When there are such facilities, such as, for example, a shared mainframe computer, attribution of the costs to individual accounts is complicated and expensive.

I should make it quite clear that my remarks were for one particular department in one particular university and one given period. Private universities, such as the Ivy League colleges, are different from the state universities and present-day practices in British universities are quite different from those at Cambridge in the 1950s. For one thing, few of today's British universities existed fifty years ago and in the meantime we have moved towards American models.

I found it a little difficult to get going with practical work. I had been advised by Francis Crick, whom I had consulted, to use the small-angle X-ray scattering apparatus in Madison to study the structure of ribosomes, the material responsible for conveying genetic information. For that project, I needed a local collaborator who was familiar with the apparatus and with chemical methods of isolating and purifying biological materials. But, whenever I raised the subject, I sensed an awkwardness. In the end, I realised that one of my Madison friends wanted to make the study of ribosomes his main project, which he did not really want to share with anyone else. For the time being his teaching duties did not allow him to engage on a major research project. Accordingly, I spent some of my time in learning biochemical techniques; I soon found that chemical manipulations were not my strong point and that my preference would always lie in the borderland between physics and engineering; that is, in the designing of new instruments and apparatus, which is what I have been able to do most of my working life. Instrument design has been defined as finding an elegant solution tomorrow to yesterday's problems; I hope that I have succeeded in avoiding falling into that trap too often. I soon spent an increasing amount of time on the design of the Royal Institution linear diffractometer and I bombarded David Phillips and the RI workshops with my drawings. Later, I squared my conscience towards the University of Wisconsin, who were paying my salary, by investigating a virus, but my results were not readily interpretable and were never published.

In April, I escaped the Madison winter, flew to New York to visit several laboratories and to see some friends and came back via Washington. I saw the Easter Sunday parade on Fifth Avenue in New York and the cherry blossom in Washington and went to a number of museums. I returned to Madison with a much rosier view of the USA especially as, during my week's absence, summer, not just spring, had arrived. From then on, one could sit outside until the midday heat or the evening mosquitoes drove one inside. I joined the University Sailing Club and spent at least an hour of every day on the lake. The mosquitoes never went far from the shore. I also went further afield and twice joined a group of people who introduced me to the thrills of white-water canoeing in aluminium canoes in northern Wisconsin.

I felt a good deal happier after the end of the claustrophobia that was the result of having been so much confined indoors by the weather. I think my American colleagues felt very much the same. Their ambition was to be taken for outdoor workers; to reveal an interest in intellectual pursuits was just not done. I was once nearly involved in a fight when I referred to attitudes, 'that we all shared with other intellectuals'. 'Liberal' became a term of opprobrium and President Reagan was later quoted as having said: 'the American people knows what liberalism is and does not like it'. Political conversations were always best avoided until the barriers created by a common language had been cleared.

My freedom was further enhanced when I acquired a magnificent second-hand Pontiac automobile from a departing Italian post-doc. This was the best bargain in automobiles that I have ever struck: it cost me $170, I drove 12,000 miles in it without any troubles, and I sold it seven months later for $120. My first journey in my car was to the International Union of Crystallography Congress in Montreal, where I gave a couple of papers and took my seat as the newly elected member of the Apparatus Commission of the Union. Before the Congress I visited Ottawa, which seemed utterly English, and then made a side trip to Niagara. After the Congress I drove with two English friends into the Laurentian mountains and then eastward along the north shore of the Gaspé peninsula. The ethnic frictions in the province of Quebec were everywhere very much in evidence. In Montreal, a dozen of us from different countries went out to a restaurant where we had to split up into two tables. It so happened that our table ordered in French and the other in English; we were served forty minutes before our colleagues. Some of my Parisian friends had considerable difficulty in understanding the Quebecquois dialect. Many years later, Valerie and I, during a holiday in the Vendée in France, met a young man who was just about to go off on another business visit to Quebec. I asked him whether he had any language difficulties there, but he told me that at the time of the French Revolution the Vendée had been one of the last royalist strongholds from where they had, in the end, fled to Canada. The Quebecquois and the present–day Vendée dialects are still very close.

I found Canada fascinating. One of the organised tours from the Congress in Montreal was to the excavation site for one of the huge locks of the St Lawrence Seaway, which was then under construction. A complete contrast was to drive somewhere near Chicoutimi in the Laurentians, where we stayed in a small township that was very much like any other American township, but was the northern end of civilisation: there were no roads and no sizeable settlements between where we were and the North Pole.

I returned to Madison after a 3500-mile trek via New Brunswick, Maine, and upper New York State. I have described this journey rather fully because I have been able to refresh my memory by re-reading the weekly letters that I sent to my mother. There were sixty-one letters by the end of the year. It never occurred to me to telephone home; a private phone call at that time was reserved for dire emergencies only and of course this was in the days before email.

I may not have achieved very much in science during my sabbatical year but I certainly managed to see a lot of North America. After only a few weeks in Madison, I set off again by car to the western United States, travelling through the South Dakota Badlands, Wyoming, and Yellowstone National Park to Salt Lake City, Utah. I had travelling companions as far as the Great Salt Lake in the form of a Swiss physicist and his wife, who left me in Utah to proceed by Greyhound bus to California while I turned back east alone. In a motel just outside Salt Lake City I got into conversation with two hitchhiking students who had been working in Alaska during the summer vacation and were now on their way back to St. Paul, Minnesota. Yielding to the strong advocacy to their good characters by the little Mormon bar maid, I offered to give them a lift the next day. They proved to be delightful companions and I finished by driving them all the way home to Minnesota, a mere 1000 miles. I was most hospitably received by one of my hitchhikers' families. It helped to be able to converse a little haltingly in Norwegian with his grandmother, a Scandinavian, like most Minnesotans. I was put up for the night and the next day taught to water-ski on the Mississippi. I was bullied unmercifully by my friend's teenaged sister who took me in hand to such good effect that in the end I managed to stay up for five minutes. So much for the dire warnings that you should never, never pick up a hitchhiker in North America unless you were prepared to be robbed and murdered.

I had to get back to be ready for my next jaunt. I had been

invited to join five others from the physics department for a two week canoe trip in the road-less area in the Quetico Park in southern Ontario, north of Duluth. This is an uninhabited wilderness of virgin forest, lakes and rivers only accessible by canoe and inhabited by bear, moose, wolves, skunks, and beavers. All food for the duration of the trip had to be brought in. This consisted mostly of dried food that had to be reconstituted. Tins were out so as to keep the weight down during the many portages, which were pretty arduous in the virgin forest. But fish were plentiful and, with keen fishermen in the party, we had plenty of delicious fresh fish every day for either breakfast or dinner. I shared a light two-man tent with one member of the party who was nearly as soft as I was. The others merely spread ground sheets under and over their sleeping bags when it rained. I was tremendously impressed by the professionalism of my companions, who had fully developed the art of keeping everything dry even if the canoe capsized in the rapids. Preparations included pouring candle wax into boxes of kitchen matches and keeping supplies of salt and sugar in hermetic film cans. In spite of their ruggedness, my friends were sufficiently American to carry a full complement of vitamin pills and skin ointments. If ever I am shipwrecked on a desert island, I would want to choose as my companions wood-crafty Midwestern Americans.

The timing of our trip had been very carefully picked. The ideal time to arrive is two days after the first frost has killed all the mosquitoes, which would make life hell in the summer. Fortunately, in the middle of this vast continent, climatic predictions are very reliable and the first frost and the first thaw can be foretold with great precision.

The trip was tough but it was an unforgettable experience. We were in the midst of beavers and their nests and dams, the highest more than six feet high. We heard bear and wolves and saw their spoors (they are not dangerous to humans in the summer when they are not short of food). We saw a vast variety of waterfowl and a moose bull crossed the lake in front of us. The night sky was magnificent and on several nights we had a marvellous display of the Northern Lights. During the two weeks we passed one other canoe and the only other stranger we met was a fire watcher who was living in a wooden lookout tower, from which he could give radio warnings of fires within a large area. He seemed quite content in his loneliness but pleased to see new faces when we climbed up the ladder to his eyrie.

Just after our return, the university was gripped by 'registration', a fantastically complex process for staff and students and which took about a week. As there was no uniform entrance standard as in Britain, every student's level was different and every case was treated differently after endless conferences between students and faculty advisors. There was an influx of some 3000 new and 12,000 old students, many of them brought by parents (for whom the union arranged a special programme) and every shop, restaurant and parking space in Madison was crowded with people.

On 4 October, 1957, there occurred an event that had a profound influence on American thinking and that greatly affected the planning of scientific and technological education and the funding of research and development projects: the Russians launched Sputnik, the first manmade satellite. Its beeping did more than to give rise to the story that each time the satellite passed over California, half the remotely controlled garage doors opened and closed. The news was received in America with shock and consternation; 'how is it', was the universal question, 'that the achievement of being the first nation in space does not belong to the USA, by now well-known to lead in every field in science and technology, but to the Russians, whose advances in engineering were due entirely to their effective espionage network? Had this enabled them to copy American progress?'

To make matters worse, a month later, the Russians launched Sputnik II, which carried a much heavier payload, taking a live dog called Laika into space and bringing him back safely. The speed with which Americans recovered from the shock was enormously impressive. Within a few days, the general response was that mistakes had been made in the teaching of science and engineering and in the organisation and coordination of research; these mistakes must be identified and corrected. Before Sputnik, visiting foreign scientists in the US were often somewhat dismayed that their hosts had so very little interest in the ways in which things were done in their home countries. If things were different in foreign countries then, almost by definition, they were inferior to American practices. This attitude changed almost overnight and, as a visitor, one was now asked: 'what can we learn from you, so that it does not happen again that we are overtaken by other nations?'

The effect was fascinating to observe and, of course, it did not take long before the American space effort had left Russian achievements behind. The first American satellite was smaller than the two Sputniks, but it was launched the next spring and NASA, the National Aeronautics and Space Administration, came into being less than a year after the launch of Sputnik I.

My own experiences in this connection were amusing. One of my hitchhiking friends from Minnesota was the secretary of the science club in his upstate Lutheran college. In this official capacity he had invited me to give a talk to his society on 'Education in Britain'. The engagement was on a day two weeks after the launch of Sputnik. I drove over, expecting an audience of a dozen or so, but found that most of the students and three quarters of the faculty were filling the hall. I spoke for forty-five minutes and was then asked questions for as long again.

I was now coming to the end of my time in Madison and could take stock of what I had learnt. I suppose that mostly I had found what I was not suited for. In experimental work I was definitely too clumsy to do well with the biochemical techniques used for the extraction and purification of biological materials. How glad I was that I was never involved in getting myoglobin from seal meat, as was one of my RI colleagues!

I left Madison in early January 1958, in weather just as cold as on my arrival a year before, but I was cheered by the warmth of the wishes that sent me on my way and by the memory of the tremendous hospitality I had received, very little of which I was ever able to repay.

I visited the USA every two or three years after my return from Madison and I had a good opportunity of observing how rapidly things were altering. Changes in race relations seemed to be noticeable between one visit and the next. In 1957, the

University of Wisconsin was very proud of the fact that it had just abandoned the requirement for students applying for admission to submit a photograph. I did not immediately realise why this was such a liberal change of policy until it was pointed out to me that without a photo no one could tell whether the applicant was black or white. (The proportion of black students in Madison was, in fact, quite small.) On my next visit I noticed in New York that the models in the windows of department stores alternated white-black-white-black with great regularity. A few years later the lack of discrimination seemed to have become much less self-conscious.

A less positive change was the increase in drug use. On early visits, I do not remember seeing anyone obviously under the influence of drugs; later, I was once the only one in a Greyhound waiting room not clearly drugged. Equally, the increase in obesity amongst college students was easily observable from visit to visit.

The stranger to the USA is often defeated by the rate at which new gadgets are introduced. Who has not looked in vain for a pushbutton, a winding handle, or a lever in a wash room to release a towel only to find that a new one is dispensed automatically when one holds one's hand under the issuing slot? I once had to phone the front desk in a hotel to discover how to choose between the different options available from the automatic coffee percolator in my room.

With my recollection of a very pleasant ocean crossing the other way, I conceived the somewhat crazy idea of going back to Europe by Italian Lines on the recommendation of a not very well informed travel agent. The *Vulcania* sailed from New York to Trieste via Boston, Lisbon, Gibraltar, Barcelona, Naples, Messina, and Patras. The final destination suited me very well, as my mother and I had arranged to meet in Gstaad in Switzerland for a few days' holiday together before the start of work in earnest. The last week of the journey in the Mediterranean was effectively a cruise, with opportunities for a few hours' sightseeing ashore at the intermediate harbours.

I was a little surprised when I arrived at the *Vulcania's* dock in New York to find the head steward allocating cabins and dining room tables from a trestle table set out at the dockside. My request for table companions speaking English, French, or German was greeted with a broad grin. I soon found out that on a three-class ship, tourist class was effectively steerage class, with tables set up in what was the refrigerated hold during the ship's summer season cruises. My table companions turned out to be an Italian seaman and a central European peasant woman, neither of whom spoke any English, two Portuguese, whose Brooklyn accents made them almost incomprehensible, and an ancient American, who became equally incomprehensible when he trod on his dentures on the first day out. At dinner, I asked my Portuguese neighbour how long he had been in the States and where?

'Dirteen years,' came the answer. 'When I got dere, I had a liddle trouble wid a knife an' I got sent up to de state pen.' It slowly dawned on me that he was being repatriated after thirteen years in the state penitentiary. The only other public room was a very small saloon, which was ruled over by a Mrs Capone and her party. I never asked her what her husband's occupation had been.

After we left Boston, I sought out the head steward and asked him how much he wanted to transfer me to the second class. The amount turned out to be quite modest and, of course, went straight into the steward's pockets. But the effect was that I found myself in elegant surroundings and pleasant company with excellent and ample food at every meal. We, again, had a very rough crossing until Lisbon, but I did not complain that the lifeboat drill was therefore postponed until we came into the Mediterranean.

I thoroughly enjoyed myself, especially the Mediterranean cruise at the end. Unfortunately, I have never had the time to cross the Atlantic by liner again.

After ten days in Switzerland, skiing for me and sunbathing for my mother, I was more than happy to get back to London and to work.

My father, E J Arndt, during the First World War, 1917.

German bank note and postage stamps during the inflation, 1922.

My mother taking me for a walk, 1926. This illustrates how few cars were on the road.

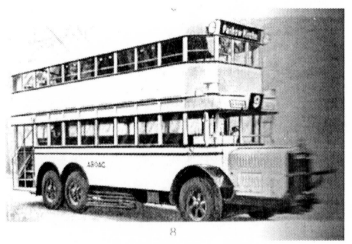

Berlin double-decker bus c.1926

German handwriting: Immer in das Zimmer.

At Dulwich College, 1936.

Undergraduate at Emmanuel College, Cambridge, 1942.

Emmanuel College XII Club Dinner, 1945. As president I am next to the master, T S Hele. The Senior Tutor, E Welbourne is two places to my left.

Cavendish Laboratory, 1945. In the front row, Henry Lipson is third from the right, G F C Searle is fifth and Professor Sir Lawrence Bragg sixth. I am immediately behind Searle and Bragg.

The fifty-kilowatt rotating anode X-ray at the Royal Institution.

Gillray, Cartoon of a Discourse *at the Royal Institution, 1802 (Very little has changed since then.)*

Skiing in the Klein Walser Tal, 1951. Note the strange bindings and the sealskins round my middle to aid climbing.

'Enjoying' a stiff breeze in mid-channel aboard a chartered yacht, 1953.

John Kendrew and Max Perutz building a model of the haemoglobin molecule, 1963.

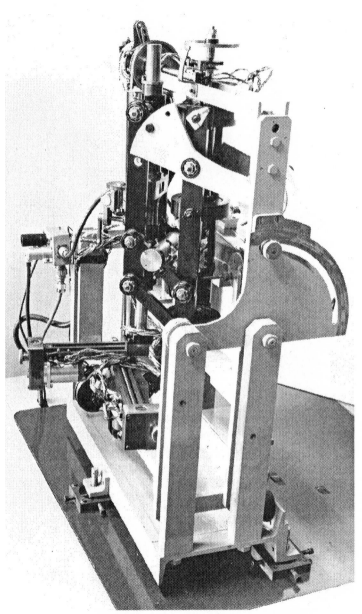

The laboratory prototype linear diffractometer, 1958.

The commercial version of the linear diffractometer by Hilger and Watts Ltd, 1961.

I demonstrate the rotation camera to Peder Kierkegaard.

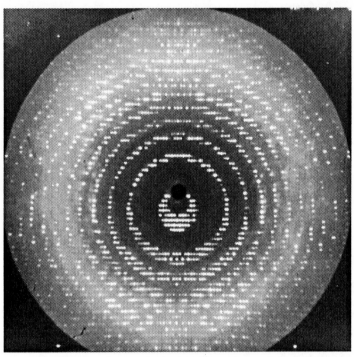

An X-ray diffraction photograph of a dehydrogenase crystal. Each bright spot is the X-ray reflection from a set of internal planes in the crystal. The structure of the molecule can be calculated from the intensities of the spots. Some hundreds of thousands of reflections may have to be measured.

Adjusting my first three-circle X-ray diffractometer.

Inspecting the punched paper output of the diffractometer, 1956.

Winter view from my room in the Faculty Club in Madison, 1957.

John Anderegg and Paul Kaesberg at -3°F on the Madison Campus.

Ed Miller, Harry Worthington, myself, and Dick Dexter, camping in the Quetico National Park in Southern Ontario, 1957.

Dick provided us with plenty of fresh fish.

Valerie and I returning from the skiing holiday in Lech, where we met, in 1955.

Wedding photograph, 29 July 1958. From left to right: Angela Parkhurst, my mother, myself, Valerie, Valerie's mother, sister Stefanie, and father. Toria Hackforth-Jones in front.

Our house in Cambridge.

Sailing with Caroline and Dick; off the Needles, Isle of Wight, 2001.

Valerie and I in St Petersburg. our last foreign holiday, 2002.

The prototype microfocus X-ray tube.

Royal Institution and marriage, 1958–1963

Good progress had been made on our instrument during my absence. Tom Faulkner, the head of the RI workshop, had made prototype versions of the mechanical linkages that David Phillips and I had designed in our exchange of letters and drawings and it did not take long to show that the instrument would work with sufficient precision to make automatic measurements of the X-ray reflections from protein crystals. I could now concentrate on fitting motors and on devising electronic controls for these motors. We were helped in patenting our design by the National Research Development Corporation (NRDC), a government-financed body with the function of assisting the turning of ideas from pure research laboratories into commercially viable and profitable products. They also helped us in our negotiations with the scientific instrument industry to find a suitable firm to manufacture our machine under licence.

I was a little disappointed to find that there was so little expertise in industry of the successful commercialisation and marketing of a new instrument. Three possible licensees underestimated the appropriate selling price of our instrument by factors of between three and seven. But then, at that time, research laboratories had little experience of buying costly instruments to accelerate their work and make it more efficient. They and the funding agencies needed educating as much as the manufacturers, who did not yet know how to build a complicated scientific instrument to an affordable price, and were yet to design into it a freedom from frequent failures and a reliability that they had so far experienced only in military equipment, where cost was less important. I shall come back to this problem later.

In addition to my laboratory work I had other important preoccupations. I had sent a Christmas card from Madison to Valerie Hilton-Sergeant without, however, telling her when I was due to return. My card was forwarded to her in South Africa, where she was spending three months with her aunt who was married to a farmer in the Orange Free State. On her return to London, she telephoned the RI to find out my American address and was put straight through to me. 'She sounded important,' said the porter who had answered the phone. After two or three meetings, I asked Valerie whether she would like to come with me in my newly acquired car to visit Cambridge, where I had to go to an important lecture by Max Perutz. I never went to the lecture: during lunch at the Bath Hotel I asked Valerie to marry me and, after some hesitation, I was accepted. Our daughters have always told everyone that Daddy had proposed to Mummy in the bath.

The next day, I called on my future father-in-law, who was then the medical adviser to the Red Cross in his office and asked for his daughter's hand in marriage. When I left, probably floating at least a foot above the floor, the secretary burst into my father-in-law's office and said, 'I smell a romance.'

It took us quite a while to enlighten our friends: mine were all convinced that I had fallen for a scheming American girl, whereas Valerie's friends thought that, with my name, I must be an Afrikaner.

Our period of engagement, which lasted only two months, passed in a whirlwind. My mother moved into a smaller flat just off Kensington Church Street, round the corner from our existing flat, which was turned into married quarters 'until we have a child'. We lived there for nearly five years, with Valerie gamely saying that negotiating sixty-five steps up to the flat with at first one and then two babies strengthened her legs for skiing holidays.

We had a wonderful wedding. Jim Hackforth-Jones, as my best man, looked after me most carefully. A friend of his family, who had been given a sleeping draught instead of a pick-me-up on the morning of his wedding to recover from his stag party, had gone to sleep on a bench in St James Park and missed his wedding. Jim made certain that nothing like that should happen to me and checked up on me by phone many times before the service. In his speech at the reception, Jim read out a recent scientific paper of mine 'to show Valerie's family how clever the bridegroom was' and had us all in stitches. I had never realised how silly a learned communication sounds when read out of context. We spent our honeymoon in Scotland and drove leisurely to the Mull of Kintyre, leaving the planning of the remainder until then. The receptionist in the hotel there said to me: 'Ye must go to Iona and your marriage will be blessed with offspring.' We did and it was. We never dared to go back to that numinous island to find out how much of the magic came from the island and how much from our euphoria. The only snag was that we were staying in the Island Hotel, owned by Mrs Campbell, so that Mrs Macdonald, who ran the general store, would not sell me any cigarettes and I had to go over to Mull to buy a fresh supply.

The blessing was so effective that Elizabeth was born ten months later in St Mary Abbots Hospital in Kensington.

We were very spoilt in those years. We were always welcome for weekends at Picket Wood, Valerie's parents' house in Merstham, and this was especially useful since, at that time, I had to make frequent trips abroad. In London, my mother was a little too ready to invite us to her flat for a meal, as she was convinced that I was not getting enough to eat while Valerie was learning to cook. Later, my mother was an ever-willing babysitter.

We had had some difficulty in finding an NHS doctor. Valerie's father got her an appointment with a Red Cross colleague who was in a South Kensington practice, but he passed her on to his partner to tell her that their panel was full. At the last moment the latter asked Valerie whether she was related to Uli Arndt: 'he was an Emmanuel man and I had supervised him in physics for his first MB', and so we were taken on.

One journey on which I was not very keen was to a conference in Stockholm that also involved a meeting of the Apparatus Commission of the International Union of Crystallography, of which I was still a member. A fellow member offered to make all the travel and hotel arrangements via his employer's travel office. I discovered too late that my colleague did not like flying and had booked surface transportation. Worse, we only found out on the boat train that he had proudly booked us into the cheapest hotel in Stockholm, which was called 'Frälshingsarmeen Hostellet'. The accommodation in the Salvation Army hostel (for that is what is was) was not bad, if you did not object to being woken up by the band at 6.30 a.m. The meeting of the Commission was a stormy one, the American chairman being at daggers drawn with both the German and the French delegates. As I was the only member who spoke all three languages, I was elected translator and all the insults were shouted at me for transmission.

At another commission meeting in Marseilles some years later, I was more successful in achieving unanimity. One of the problems of a gathering in a city foreign to all the members is that someone will always propose eating in a restaurant at the greatest possible distance away. At this meeting, I had noticed a slightly sinister greasy spoon dive just round the corner from my hotel. I persuaded the others that I knew of a very unpretentious looking place, which, however, served the best bouillabaisse in Marseilles and led my colleagues to the little bar which had just enough seats for the five of us, from Britain, USA, Australia, Sweden, and the USSR. Such is the power of suggestion that they all agreed that they had been served the best bouillabaisse ever. I clearly remember the conversation over the meal when we Westerners all mentioned our worries over our children's chances of getting into the universities of their choice. Not so our Russian friend, who announced with a broad grin, 'When I want my son to go to a certain university he gets in, of course.'

The other thing I remember about the Marseilles meeting is that the late ending of the last session left me with very little time to get to the airport to catch my plane. When I asked the taxi driver whether he could make it in time he said: 'Monsieur, any other driver in Marseilles would say "impossible", but me, I am a rally driver also, and I can do it.'

I was then treated to a most hair-raising exhibition of driving in which we cornered on two wheels and jumped the division between the road and the service road at the side. Meanwhile, my driver assured me that he found *les Anglais* at the rallies *trés sympathiques,* because they were always so *décontractés*. I got to the airport, not so *décontracté*, but with enough time to buy a paperback novel to read on the plane.

We made good progress with our diffractometer in the lab and it was not too long before it was placed in front of an X-ray tube and a crystal was mounted in position. I could have gone on for quite a while, making improvements to the instrument, but David

Phillips, true to Voltaire's maxim that the better is the enemy of the good, started making measurements on a crystal of myoglobin straight away. We proudly showed off our diffractometer to John Kendrew on his next visit to the lab. He was duly impressed and wanted to know whether we had yet given a demonstration to Max Perutz and said that, when we did, Max's first question would be whether we had put on a crystal of haemoglobin. When Max came the next week, he inspected the instrument most carefully and then asked, 'have you tried it with a crystal of haemoglobin?' (The molecule of haemoglobin on which Max Perutz was working was four times as large as the molecule of myoglobin of which John Kendrew determined the structure, and was thus even more of a challenge.)

It did not take me very long to realise that, while we had a viable instrument in our linear diffractometer, in the long run, the instrument of the future was the four-circle diffractometer, which I had started to design. This was because it was already becoming clear that digital computers were getting cheaper and that, before long, every laboratory would have access to its own computer, which could be used to control scientific instruments, so that one would then not need to build a special-purpose computer into an instrument, as we had effectively done in the linear diffractometer.

About this time, I ran into Terry Willis, an old friend from Cambridge days, who was then working on neutron diffraction at the Atomic Energy Research Establishment (AERE) at Harwell. The practice of neutron diffraction was as much politics-driven as science-driven: the prospects of atomic energy, not to mention the need for atomic weapons, required the building of reactors of all types; reactors produced neutrons and neutrons could be used for structural studies, just like X-rays, by measuring the neutrons diffracted, or scattered, by crystalline materials. Very interesting results had been obtained in some fields but in others, notably in the study of biological substances, it was not clear to me that the efforts that had been devoted to neutron diffraction had been justified. The same information could have been obtained more quickly and more cheaply by other methods. I made myself less than popular at a French meeting on neutron diffraction from proteins when I could not resist coming out with an inversion of

Voltaire's *bon mot* about God by saying '*Si le neutron n'existait pas, il ne serait pas nécessaire de l'inventer*', if the neutron did not exist, it would not be necessary to invent it.

Whatever the merits, a fair amount of money had been spent on neutron diffraction and on the engineering effort required in that field and I remarked to my friend, Terry Willis, that it was strange that so little work had been done on developing automatic instrumentation for neutron diffraction, to make the most efficient use of the neutron supply, when, in the less generously funded field of X-ray crystallography, several other laboratories apart from ours at the RI were building automatic diffractometers. Terry's response was, 'Why don't you come to Harwell, perhaps as a vacation consultant, and design such an instrument for us?'

The offer was a tempting one for two reasons: there was a large staff of engineers at Harwell who were somewhat under-employed because the pressure to develop atomic energy was much less than when AERE was first set up. These engineers were available to do much of the humdrum part of the design work. Besides, any developments of neutron diffractometers would immediately help to improve X-ray diffractometers, which to me and, I hoped, the general scientific community, was more important.

As a result of our efforts, there were produced, more or less in parallel, an automatic neutron, and an automatic X-ray, diffractometer. The shaft-setting electronics was made by the Ferranti Numerical Control Division in Edinburgh and was an adaptation of what they were selling for automating workshop machinery such as milling machines and lathes. The mechanical part of both instruments was very similar and was built by Hilger and Watts, then a leading manufacturer of optical and X-ray instruments. The diffractometers were made under licence from AERE, who had taken out a patent in the joint names of Arndt and Willis; the instrument was marketed by the two companies in combination.

The diffractometer was a world first and gave the two industrial partners a lead of at least two years over any other similar instrument on the market. Yet, although a fair number was sold, the diffractometer was not the success it deserved to be. This was partly because some corners had been cut: I remember the first technical discussion with the Ferranti team when one of their engineers outlined a possible design, only to be stopped by the commercial manager who said, 'Hold on, you are not designing for the military now and you must use sixpenny instead of shilling diodes.' The result was that the completed instrument had more frequent failures than it should have had. In addition, the marketing was too slow and not sufficiently aggressive.

One frequently sees it stated that British scientists have good ideas but lack the ability to turn them into practical ventures. My own experience, and that of colleagues who have invented novel scientific instruments, is that the scientists' advice on commercialisation is too often ignored and that it is the manufacturers who do not do their own job well enough.

In order to achieve adequate collaboration on the designing, I spent several weeks in two successive summers at Harwell. The three of us, our daughter Elizabeth was born just before our first visit, were put up both times in Buckland House, the stately home of the Wellesley family, which AERE had rented as a hostel for visiting scientists and their families. We all enjoyed the rural surroundings, especially our baby. The summer weather in 1959 and 1960 remains in my memory as being particularly fine. I learnt two lessons that summer: how difficult laboratory work is when one is tied to a rigidly fixed bus timetable and how important it is for safety precautions to be fail-safe. The buses that conveyed the staff to and from the laboratory mostly crept along the Berkshire roads with their high hedges and sharp corners. However, there was one driver who had an arrangement with a friend who always sat in the front of the upper deck, from where he could see oncoming traffic over the top of the hedges. Only when the friend stamped on the floor when he saw oncoming traffic did the driver slow down before a blind corner. Alas, one day the watcher was missing and, in the absence of a signal, the bus ran straight into an oncoming van. I believe that after that the signal was changed to one where stamping meant 'road clear'.

In September 1960 our second daughter, Caroline, was born at home in our flat. There was then a great shortage of maternity beds in hospitals. When I brought out a bottle of gin to toast the safe arrival and apologised for not having any tonic water, the midwife reminded me indignantly that surely I had some National Orange Juice, which was then handed out free to babies. The mixture turned out to be an adequate and, presumably, a healthy substitute for gin and orange.

The laboratory at the RI was a busy and happy place. We worked in close collaboration with Max Perutz's and John Kendrew's Cambridge team and joined in the celebrations of some of their successes, such as in the party at Peterhouse where John demonstrated the first interpretable map of myoglobin. We had driven over complete with baby, whose carrycot was parked in John's bedroom and whose gentle snoring caused one of the guests to ask whether he was allowed to keep a cat in his rooms.

Sir Lawrence and Lady Bragg, who occupied the director's flat above the public part of the RI, treated us as part of the family. There were summer outings to their country cottage at Waldringfield, a skating party on the pond in St James Park, and we were invited to Patience Bragg's wedding. Many of the discourses and afternoon lectures for school children, which Sir Lawrence had by now instituted to give a new purpose to the RI, were great fun to watch. He was a most entertaining lecturer, who could keep his adult and juvenile audiences spellbound. One of his tricks was to draw a perfect freehand circle on the blackboard, having first located the centre. I only discovered many years later from his niece, Lady Adrian, that he achieved this feat by drawing the circle on the board in pencil before the lecture and tracing the invisible line with chalk.

Many tricks were employed in the lectures to good effect: in the model of a molecule, certain parts were painted with fluorescent paint and the lecturer could draw attention to them at the appropriate moment by switching on a source of ultraviolet light, which made the painted parts shine brightly. This particular demonstration was not popular with the good-looking lecture assistant, who had an artificial central front tooth: under ultraviolet illumination her natural teeth fluoresced brightly but the artificial one remained a dark gap. During the televising of one of the professor's lectures, Philip Daly, the BBC producer, said to us that, given a little time, he could turn Bragg into a first class television personality. It did not seem to occur to him that that would not necessarily be the professor's highest ambition.

I had several other encounters with the media. At one time, a television team descended on our laboratory to record our X-ray equipment for a schools programme on 'Energy'. In those days, every team seemed to have several producers called Algernon and Clarence, with several production assistants called Olga and Sonia. All the hard work was done by an obviously ex-RN petty officer called Bill. When the rest of the team could not find a position for their spotlights that did not cause awkward reflections from the front panels of my racks of electronics, Bill disappeared round the corner into Old Bond Street and returned with a set of Max Factor matt stage make-up, which he applied liberally to the panels and which totally suppressed the reflections.

I was invited to a television auditorium for the preview of the completed film in front of the editorial team and the science adviser. The film started with a beautiful shot of seagulls soaring above thundering waves, while a voice intoned: 'Energy. Energy is Power and Power is Energy'. When the lights came on again at the end, the producer asked for comments. When all he received were some fairly irrelevant remarks, I said, 'You are presumably going to alter the opening words.'

'Why?'

'Because power is energy per unit time and you cannot start an educational film with a statement that every schoolboy would know to be wrong.'

Much to my surprise, I was not offered the science adviser's job then or at any time later.

I do not know why I was once invited to give a radio talk on the metric system. It was a live broadcast but I had to read my talk from a manuscript, which I had to hand to the producer before. Sir Lawrence Bragg, who was a very accomplished and frequent broadcaster, advised me to alter the odd word here and there, such as to change a 'therefore' to a 'thus', or a 'rapidly' to a 'quickly'. This would cause a very slight hesitation which would make the talk sound much more natural. I have occasionally used this trick in lectures where I had to speak from a prepared script, but I have never made another broadcast.

I remember, with some embarrassment, a brick which I dropped. I had been showing a party of young Germans round the RI. They stopped in front of the large painting of Sir William Bragg, the professor's father, and wanted to know who it was. I explained that Sir William had for many years been the director of the RI and that now his son was the director.

'*Ach ja,*' they said 'it is just like Germany. You must have family influence to get anywhere.'

Knowing, like all scientists, that the son was a greater man than his father, I told the story as a good joke to the professor, who was not at all amused. It was only later that I discovered from the biography of Sir William Bragg by his daughter that it was a sore point with her brother that the world gave some of the credit to his father for work that he had done. Max Perutz told me that Bragg congratulated him on an academic success of Robin, Max's son, and particularly on the fact that Robin had chosen a field at some remove from his father's, 'which,' said Bragg, 'is always a good thing.'

In 1962, my Dewar fellowship came to an end and I realised that I owed it to my growing family to find a tenured appointment, or at least a job with some promise of permanency. Besides, it was becoming more difficult to bring up two lively growing girls, one of whom was approaching nursery school age, in a third floor flat without a lift. I was travelling a good deal, lecturing at summer schools and giving talks about X-ray instrumentation, and the burden on Valerie was getting heavier. Then, to my astonishment and delight, Max Perutz invited me to join his laboratory, which in 1962 moved into new premises in Cambridge and became the MRC Laboratory of Molecular Biology. I became an employee of the MRC (Medical Research Council) in 1962 with the promise of tenure after a year. I remained at the RI for another year to finish off my work there but my name was on a door of the new Cambridge Laboratory, of which I was thus one of the founder members.

My swansong after fourteen years in the Davy-Faraday Laboratory of the Royal Institution was to deliver a Friday Evening Discourse. As my subject I had chosen automation in the laboratory and, with the help of lecture demonstrations, I attempted to describe a futuristic vision of laboratory experiments in which measurements of all kinds would be made by instruments directly connected to digital computers, which could then be used to process the results and provide feedback to optimise the measuring conditions. My predictions fell far short of the reality that we were to experience within a surprisingly short time span. I was generously supported by a number of manufacturers, who lent me equipment for lecture demonstrations and for the customary small exhibition in the library after the lecture. Thus Messrs Ferranti produced their latest Argus computer, which was manhandled up and down the main staircase of the RI. It was too big to fit into the lift and was then the ultimate in sophistication – it had a power less than that of a modern laptop computer. My discourse was a reasonable success, but it left me drained as no lecture I had given before or since has done.

Terry Willis and I decided to write a book together which would embody our experiences of building an X-ray and a neutron diffractometer in parallel, and which would try to compare and contrast the two techniques. Obviously, I would write the X-ray part and Terry the neutron one, but we would both be responsible jointly for the entire text with the right to criticise and, if necessary, to alter the chapters written by the other. This decision produced a coherent text, I believe easier for the reader, but it necessarily caused some friction between us, especially as our working methods were quite different: Terry believed in producing a number of drafts of each chapter and progressively revising them, whereas my method has always been to think for a long time before putting pencil to paper and then to write what is essentially the final version in one go. We also differed on points of style and grammar but I soon discovered a method of getting my own way adopted. Terry had a great respect for Valerie's opinion as an arts graduate and all I had to say was, 'Valerie thinks so and so is better.' Although I once threw the manuscript of a chapter at Terry, and although he stormed away from our house and started to drive home before he discovered that he had left his washing tackle in our bathroom, we soon got our friendship back to how it had always been. The book was finally published as a Cambridge University Press Monograph on Physical Sciences and was a reasonable success.

In order to make my part of the book fully up to date, I wanted to visit as many as possible of the American laboratories where relevant work was going on. Max readily gave me permission for this trip, as long as I did not draw on his laboratory travel allowance. I found that Messrs Hilger and Watts and Messrs Ferranti, the manufacturers of the two diffractometers, were quite prepared to foot the bill, as I was going to lecture about the instruments, and I fixed up quite a lengthy programme of visits. Then, at the last moment, Max phoned me up and told me to ring the MRC to confirm that they had no objections. I was told that they were sorry but they could not give a council employee permission to give sales talks for commercial equipment. I said in desperation that my lectures had all been fixed with my American hosts and that, in any case, I did not intend to say anything which I would not have said if my trip had been financed by the MRC. There was a lengthy pause and then the voice over the phone said, 'In that case I think that we should pay for the trip', and they did. This incident was typical of the broad-minded and non-bureaucratic way in which the MRC took their decisions in those happy days and tried to meet the wishes of their staff if they were at all reasonable.

I spent five interesting and profitable weeks visiting a large number of laboratories and crossing the United States from east to west and from north to south. I was left with the impression that the X-ray instrumentation that we were developing in Britain and, in particular, the shaft-setting methods used in the diffractometers that were being built by Hilger and Watts and Ferranti Numerical Control Division, were superior to any commercially available instruments in America. I was keen to tell these companies my impression of the possibilities of new markets. The Ferranti people had wanted to pay me a consultancy fee but at that time MRC staff were not allowed to act as consultants. As a consolation, Ferranti sent me a first class return ticket to Edinburgh and invited me to lunch in a good restaurant in Princes Street.

Knowing that I would get a good breakfast on the plane, I had nothing to eat before setting off for the air terminal but, just after takeoff, there was an announcement that because of exceptional turbulence no breakfast would be served. A second message was that, because of heavy crosswinds, we could not land in Edinburgh but would try to land in Glasgow. That attempt was also cancelled and we were taken to Prestwick. I did at least manage to get a bar of chocolate from a slot machine while waiting for the buses that took us to Edinburgh. I arrived in Princes Street just in time to see my well-dined and wined hosts emerging from the restaurant. During the discussions in the afternoon, I consoled myself with the prospect of the first-class dinner on the return flight in the evening but, alas, the cross wind was still blowing hard and BEA regretfully announced that the Vanguard to London had to be replaced with a smaller and more manoeuvrable Viscount aircraft, which would be one class only, where no meals would be served. Passengers with first-class tickets were given forms for claiming a refund. The refund was, of course, payable to Messrs Ferranti, who had bought the ticket. I was rather hungry when I arrived home on just one small chocolate bar since the previous evening's supper.

LMB, Cambridge and ILL, Grenoble, 1963–1973

On my return from the United States in 1963, we started to house hunt in Cambridge in earnest and found a house in a new development in Little Shelford, only three miles from the laboratory, in attractive rural surroundings. After living in London, we found it wonderful to be able to stroll across a meadow on the banks of the Cam and to sit under the trees watching the minnows in the water at our feet. Traffic in and around Cambridge at that time was still quite light. I could drive along a country road from home to the lab, only taking care to avoid the rabbits on the way, and park the car just outside my office window. Forty years later, the hospital site on which the MRC laboratory was one of the first buildings had been filled to such an extent that car parking was only permitted in designated places, where we had to pay for the privilege of driving to work.

Cambridge seemed to have stood still in the fifteen years since I had finished as a research student. I still recognised many of the shop assistants and it was a common experience to be greeted by an elderly don in the market place with the words: 'I have not seen you for some time, have you been away?' When I went to have my hair cut in the same place to which I had gone as a research student, the barber said to me, 'It is quite a while since I last cut your hair, sir.' I felt immensely flattered until I discovered that this was his standard phrase for any middle-aged man whom he did not immediately recognise.

The Medical Research Council Laboratory of Molecular Biology was the most stimulating place. It was only later that it came to be called the LMB. In the early days, it was always referred to as 'the MRC', especially by Americans. At the time of the celebration of the twenty-fifth anniversary of the founding of the laboratory in 1987, Sir James Gowans, the secretary of the Medical Research Council, made a speech in which he showed a certain resentment that when he described himself as the secretary of the MRC in the USA, Americans tended to assume that he was at the

LMB. Dogs do not like being wagged by their tails!

I think we all realised what a privilege it was to be working in that unique and lively atmosphere. Red tape was kept to an absolute minimum and administration was entirely in the hands of Audrey Martin and Michael Fuller, who was, and remained for forty years, an active and knowledgeable laboratory steward, for whom nothing was too much trouble. Audrey's dog, Slippers, spent the day under her desk and organisational problems tended to be more readily resolved if Slippers approved of you by wagging her tail.

There was no feeling of a hierarchy in the laboratory. Max Perutz once told me that, in deciding on tenured appointments in the lab, he tried to choose only scientists who, he thought, would one day be elected to the Royal Society. Shortly before Max retired from the chairmanship of the board of the laboratory, I heard a visiting professor say to him, 'I expect you will be glad to lay down your administrative duties in September and have more time for research.' The visitor was a little surprised by Max's reply.

'Oh, I have never found that administration took up much of my time.' This was partly explained by the enormous respect in which he was held at MRC headquarters where the attitude in those happy days was: 'If that is what Dr Perutz wants, we must see how we can satisfy him.'

The non-scientific staff of the laboratory were devoted to him. I often found that, when a staff member of the lab was ill and when I visited him or her in hospital, Max had already been there, probably more than once, and done something useful for the patient. I can do no better than to quote from a letter written to me by Joy Fordham, after I had missed the party marking her retirement from her job as manager of the laboratory staff restaurant, a position she had filled for forty years. She wrote:

> I think perhaps it is an end of an era, a new page. Dr Perutz gone, Mrs Perutz very frail. I do not think many of the younger members of the lab knew that, if it had not been for Max and Mrs Perutz, there would not have been a canteen until Aaron Klug in his speech at my party told them. I have always tried to run the canteen and to treat everyone, my staff and members of the lab, in

the way in which Max treated everyone in the lab. My one regret is that I did not thank Max for all he did for me when I was ill. I have always been very proud to have worked in the lab.

The laboratory was still sufficiently small to form a very close-knit community. We all knew more or less what everyone was doing and one could go to any seminar without being totally bewildered. Anyone who was not accustomed to the ways of the laboratory must have found it a terrifying experience to give a lecture or a seminar there. Everyone felt free to interrupt the speaker with searching questions or withering comments and to walk out if the talk failed to come up to expectations.

Sydney Brenner and Francis Crick often kept up a not so *sotto voce* commentary during seminars. I remember one talk, given by Francis himself, when he reported on a recent visit to Leslie Orgel at La Jolla, where Leslie had speculated on the synthesis of proteins in the primeval soup at catalytic sites provided by chips of the mineral appatite.

'I see,' interjected Sydney, 'chips before fish.'

Although there was no repartee on this occasion, Francis usually seemed to think faster than anyone else. There was a lab party at which we played a game in which we had to write down as many possible uses of a book as we could think of. Most people finished with about twenty but Francis was still writing furiously when he was stopped at more than a hundred uses.

John Kendrew was deputy chairman of the laboratory under Max. His quiet reticence was the greatest possible contrast to Francis' and Sydney's ebullience. John was probably the first one to realise that future advances in molecular biology required not only new techniques, especially in computation, data storage, and data retrieval, but also needed the working together of bigger teams with more collaborators than was then customary.

He assembled around him a team of extremely lively and clever post-docs, many of them American. As an excellent organiser and committee chairman, he was often away from the lab; one tended to meet strangers who, when John's name was mentioned, would say: 'Oh yes, I have met him on the submarine warfare committee,' or on some other national or international committee.

John's travels were always well planned. He was the first person

I knew who had a tape deck installed in his car. He once told me that he did most of his grocery shopping in the supermarket at Orly airport. David Phillips, himself much occupied with a multitude of committees in his later years, used to describe John Kendrew as the most effective part-time research worker he knew.

The laboratory canteen was a focal point for everyone. One sat at any table where there was an empty chair and the scientists were not outnumbered by the administrative and office staff, as was to happen later. The canteen was supervised by Gisela Perutz; visiting foreign scientists were often surprised that the lady in a white coat who dished out their vegetables was the wife of the Nobel laureate chairman of the laboratory. (Max Perutz always insisted on the title of Chairman of the Governing Body of the Laboratory, rather than 'Director').

In 1984, the government appointed the Rayner Committee, which was intended to look into the cost effectiveness of, among other bodies, Medical Research Council laboratories. The assessor, on detached duty from another MRC establishment, spent some months in our laboratory, during which time we could not understand his failure to recognise the special nature of the laboratory that made it function so well. He was clearly antagonised by what he regarded as our arrogance. When he pointed out that our travel budget per head was lower than that of other laboratories, he was told that when anyone, anywhere, had done something interesting, he would come to Cambridge to tell us about it, and that other institutions were only too ready to pay the expenses of LMB members coming to visit them to give lectures or seminars. The assessor thought that the workshops' short waiting list was indicative of overstaffing whereas, in reality, the close contacts between research staff and workshop members ensured that possible jobs were first discussed informally and action was requested only if the work could be done quickly. We were certainly arrogant but then we felt we had a lot to be arrogant about.

Our daughters, Elizabeth and Caroline, started school life in the little nursery school run by the wife of our local policeman. Among the fellow parents, I discovered Jim Long and Peter

Duncumb, whom I had met many years before in London and with whom I was to have a fruitful scientific collaboration more than thirty years later.

Both girls went on to the Shelford Village School, which was pleasant enough but where the standards seemed to us to be very low. When I went to see the headmaster, he said to me: 'Do not worry, Mr Arndt; Elizabeth will never be stretched.' I felt that this was an utter condemnation of a system of education and, in due course, we sent Elizabeth to Byron House School in Cambridge, a very well-run private school. Caroline joined her there later. She had found at the village school that, as she had learnt to read while at nursery school, she was told just to get on with her books without ever being heard. She was asked to occupy herself by teaching a boy called Philip to read and felt a strong sense of failure because Philip did not seem to be making much progress. This feeling only lifted some years later, long after she had left Shelford school, when she heard that, at the age of thirteen, Philip still could not read.

Elizabeth won a free place at the Perse School for Ggirls on the strength of her performance in the 'eleven-plus' exam. Caroline did not quite make it there and could have gone to the County High School for Girls but, as that school was to be converted into a sixth form college, Caroline's year would have been one of the last intakes into the normal school. Accordingly, we swallowed our principles and Caroline joined Elizabeth at the Perse School. When it came to Annabel's turn, she wanted to go where her sisters had gone and they backed her, so we finished up with all three at a private school.

History repeated itself in the next generation with Elizabeth's children. Edward won a place as a chorister at King's College Choir School, where the academic standards were high and appropriate for a boy who was bright as well as very musical. Helen, who was just as musical and bright, followed her mother and her aunts to the Perse School for Girls. It appears that principles of opposition to private schooling do not stand a strong chance while there are private schools that are much better than the state schools!

In the first few years after moving to Cambridge, I seem to

have done a lot of travelling: teaching at summer schools in Denmark and Holland, helping a Swiss laboratory to get used to their linear diffractometer, attending a crystallographic congress in Rome, examining a PhD candidate in Sweden, and attending other scientific meetings in Germany and France. Mostly I left Valerie at home and came back as quickly as I could; in this I differed from some of my colleagues, who turned every scientific meeting into a family outing. But Valerie came with me to Rome to a conference, during which Terry Willis and I were hauled out of a lecture by an embassy official, acting on behalf of the UK Atomic Energy Authority, who wanted our diffractometer patented before we gave our lectures and who had us taken to an Italian patent attorney. That time in Rome, we were so homesick for our daughters that we bought two very lifelike dolls for them. (None of our children ever had the slightest interest in dolls.) We were staying in a very superior hotel on the Via Veneto and I shocked Valerie when I used a false coin that I had been given in my change somewhere to tip the smarmy doorman as he handed us into our airport taxi on the last day. I felt that he would have a far better opportunity of getting rid of the coin than I.

During my many journeys, I had been the frequent target at airports and elsewhere for public opinion pollsters. I was once thanked very politely by a French Boy Scout in the Luxembourg Gardens when I was able to identify *Kim* but had to admit that I could only quote the Scout Law in English. I was stopped one day in the street in Munich by a young woman who was conducting a survey of beer consumption. When I told her, completely honestly, that my favourite beer was Younger's Scotch Ale of which I drank seven pints a year, half a pint an evening during the annual two weeks' Lake District holiday, she stomped off in disgust. I did not do very much better when I was interrogated on the train between Boulogne and Paris by a young man on behalf of SNCF, the French state railways. I had told him, again truthfully, that that year I had crossed the Channel seven times, three times by air, twice by car ferry, once by cross-channel steamer, and once by sailing yacht. I have often doubted the accuracy of polls; the wielders of the clipboards and their forms do not seem to be able to cope with the out of the ordinary!

Valerie was once stopped as she bicycled into the Addenbrooke's Hospital site in Cambridge by a side entrance and asked whether she was using that way in as a shortcut to somewhere else or whether she worked there.

'Neither,' she said, 'I am a patient.'

But there did not appear to be a space on the form for that category and she was written down as 'Visiting the hospital site for other purposes.'

It was much easier at that time to change plane tickets, or even to alter one's itinerary at the last moment. On a trip to Italy, I wanted to make such a change at Milan Airport. I presented my ticket and my request at the counter, where the clerk immediately grabbed a telephone into which he said: 'Ancona, Roma, Napoli, Domodossola, Torino.' I interrupted him that that was much too complicated a route. It was only when I tried my luck at the next counter and again heard the clerk say: 'Ancona, Roma, Napoli, Domodossola, Torino,' that I realised that they had merely been spelling my name.

It is certainly a good idea to know as much as possible about the procedures and customs of the countries that one is visiting. I appreciated the advice to bring flowers when invited to dinner in France, but on no account to make it chrysanthemums, which are used only for funerals. I was also glad that when I was asked to dinner in Sweden at 8.00 p.m., and taken the care to inquire exactly when I should present myself, I was told that the correct time was between 7.59 p.m. and 8.01 p.m. I asked my taxi driver to drop me fifty yards from my destination when I saw that I was five minutes early. I walked slowly to my host's house, conscious of being followed at snail's pace by a large Jaguar. As the clock struck on a nearby church and as I accelerated, a Saab, coming from the opposite direction, screeched to a halt in front of the door. It was as well for me that the driver of the Jaguar was the British consul, whom I could ask in his official capacity to give me a lift back to my hotel after dinner; I had only arrived late that afternoon and had not had time to change enough money to pay the fare back to town.

On another occasion, in Sweden, when I acted as a PhD examiner, I regretted my ignorance of some Swedish institutions.

As a visiting VIP I was provided with a 'nanny', in the form of a research student whose job it was to guide and assist me. On my last day, I asked him to take me to a post office, as I wanted to send a telegram to my wife. He trotted by my side, obviously far from happy. As we approached the post office, he managed to get out: 'Excuse me, but in Sweden we do not send telegrams from post offices, we send them from telegraph offices.' When I asked him to take me to such an office, he was about to summon a taxi but managed to get out. 'But why do you not want to send your telegram from the University?' (whither we were bound.)

On a visit to Moscow, I probably also offended my 'nanny' there, a chemistry post-doc whom I asked, probably too persistently, why a Russian first degree course took five years as against our three.

'You see, we do not only have lectures on chemistry. There are other subjects, also.'

'Such as?'

'History of the Revolution and dialectical materialism.'

'Oh, bad luck!'

'I have always found that my study of dialectical materialism was a great help in my research work as a chemist!'

I have a much happier Russian memory involving Nikolai Kiselev, whom I have met from time to time over a period of forty years. The first time was at a drinks party in the house of my colleague Hugh Huxley, who owned a boisterous Old English sheepdog.

'What sort of a dog is that?' I heard Nikolai asking Valerie.

'It is an Old English sheepdog.'

'Oh yes, the English must always have a dog on a ship.'

'Not ship, sheep.'

'Yes, the English are great sailors, always on a ship.'

And then, in one of those silences one sometimes gets at a party, I heard my dear wife's voice saying, 'Baah, baah.' And Nikolai has over the years when we met never failed to ask me with a smile how my wife was.

Summer schools and workshops were always a good opportunity for meeting colleagues of all levels of seniority on an informal footing. These events were often held in most attractive resorts, of course in the off-peak season. Thus, I have vivid recollections of a meeting in Sorrento, during which it never stopped raining, and of a workshop in the hill village of Erice in Sicily, when the clouds all around us parted only for brief glimpses of the sun-baked Sicilian plain below us. It was just as well that, during a winter conference in the Austrian Alps, the snow was rather sparse, so that one could not exhaust oneself skiing all morning because ski trousers are rather slippery and one tended to slide off the wooden benches during the afternoon and evening sessions, if one had taken too much exercise earlier in the day.

Sometimes it worked out very well. Valerie joined me during the last day of a summer school in Aarhus in Denmark and, having climbed Scafell Pike in the English Lake District, we now wanted to bag the highest mountain in Denmark in the Danish lake district. It took us exactly fifteen minutes to get to the top.

Once, at a meeting in the Klein-Walser Tal on the borders of Germany and Austria, the snow on the upper slopes was so good that I made three phone calls: one to book a room in Oberlech on the other side of the Arlberg, our favourite ski resort, one to my mother in London, asking her to babysit for us for a few days, and one to Valerie, persuading her to join me at Oberlech. I also got my colleague, Ken Holmes, who had come out by car, to drive me to Lech.

During a conference in Germany some years later, I got into a very lively political discussion with a group of German research students over a bottle of wine. They wanted to know why Mrs Thatcher was so opposed to a European federation. I told them that the British were the only nation in Europe who felt in no way ashamed of their record during the last war and that, as a result, a sizeable proportion of the electorate was against any loss of national sovereignty. Some months after this, Valerie and I got into conversation with an elderly gentleman on a plane to Zurich. He turned out to be Sir Bernard Braine, MP, who was taking a party of British MPs to a joint Anglo-German Parliamentary meeting. I related to him my conversation with the young Germans and it was obvious that, for all his official contacts with German parliamentarians, he had never had a frank discussion with real people.

It has always struck me that a whole generation of young Germans, approximately those born between 1945 and 1970 was very ignorant of what had happened in the Nazi era, during the war and in the early post-war period. At a time when airport and railway station bookstalls in Britain and in the USA were flooded with the memoirs of soldiers, politicians and airmen, very few books touching on life between 1918 and 1945 could be found in Germany. I shall not forget a conversation between a Hungarian scientist, a young German and myself, some years later but still before the fall of communism, when the Hungarian expressed himself fairly freely about the iniquities of the Communist regime in Hungary.

After a while he pulled himself up and said; 'I had better keep quiet or I shall find myself without a job when I get home.'

'But have you not got tenure?' the German asked.

'Yes, but what has that to do with it?'

'If you have tenure you cannot be dismissed.'

'Listen, Hans,' I said, 'In a Communist country, or for that matter in Nazi Germany, if you displeased the government you were out of a job, or imprisoned, however much tenure you had.'

'I can believe that of a Communist dictatorship, but not of Germany,' he replied.

The present generation of Germans has a very much better knowledge of recent history and a much wider range of books and paperbacks is now published and read.

The onward march of computers and the increase in their complexity was fast and inexorable. The history of the developments is an interesting one. It is doubtful whether any structures of very large molecules could have been determined without the help of digital computers. However, it took some time for the need to be realised. In 1952, Steffen Peiser proposed that the British Institute of Physics should buy a Ferranti Pegasus computer for use by the entire crystallographic community for all their computing. The suggestion was turned down because it was estimated that all crystallographers' needs could be met in one eight-hour session per day and it would be too cumbersome to set up an organisation for leasing computing time to outsiders, as would be necessary to make the operation economically feasible.

Since the mid 1950s, all scientific laboratories have had access to central 'mainframe' computers for their number-crunching computations. Input and output data were conveyed to and from the computing centres by means of decks of punched cards; the LMB employed a team of girls – known as 'computors' – who, at one time, commuted regularly between Cambridge and the London Data Centre. Our experience in attempting to use the mainframe computer, EDSAC II, for the control of our diffractometer had shown us that the long access and turn-around times made computers of this type inconvenient for this kind of work. By 1964, both the RI, which I had left in 1963, and the MRC, to which I had moved, had their own small computers, each occupying a medium-sized room, of a type expressly designed for being connected directly to experimental apparatus.

Buying a computer was a very important transaction. Messrs Ferranti sent a small plane to Cambridge to convey the purchasing committee consisting of David Blow, Herman Watson and myself to their Manchester-Wythenshaw works to demonstrate their ARGUS computer to us.

Valerie came to Cambridge airport to see us off, accompanied by Elizabeth, on their way to her nursery school. Elizabeth was terribly upset: she had seen Daddy vanishing into a dot in the sky so she thought he was on his way to heaven and never expected to see me again.

We intended to connect several instruments and other devices to our new computer. Designing and building interfaces between them and the ARGUS and writing the control programs became the major occupations for some years for Frank Mallett, who came to us from Harwell, and for Tim Gossling, whom we recruited from Ferranti. Interfacing at that time was a do-it-yourself occupation, even for such mundane devices as magnetic tape drives.

One of the first instruments that we connected to the new computer was a fine-focus cathode-ray tube, which could be used to produce graphics output of a high quality, by photographing the path traced out by the spot of light. We could also turn the device into a microdensitometer, that is, we could measure the amount of light from a small spot that was transmitted through a transparent film and thus determine the film density, at that point, with a sensitive photocell with a digital output. By repeating this procedure at a large number of very small sampling points on the film, we could read the entire image of the film into the computer. Unlike existing film scanners, which scanned the film in a raster or in a spiral, ours was a random access microdensitometer, with which we needed to look only at those points of the image where we knew important information to be and thus we could save greatly in time and computer memory.

This microdensitometer was first used by Aaron Klug and David de Rosier to digitise a series of electron microscope images, in which the virus particle under examination had been tilted in steps so that the specimen was viewed at increasing angles to the film surface. The computer could then generate a three-dimensional view of the virus from a series of projections. I asked a radiologist friend of mine whether the same technique could be useful for the whole or parts of the human body, but I was told that doctors knew the human body so well that they could locate any point of special interest from two projections at right angles. The method of using a series of tilted radiographs to obtain three-dimensional views is now known as tomography and is used in pretty well every hospital in the world.

I myself was interested in using the new microdensitometer for X-ray diffraction photographs of protein crystals. These photographs contain a large number of spots, generated when the crystal is rotated in the X-ray beam, each spot corresponding to an X-ray reflection from one particular internal plane of the crystal lattice. A very large number of such reflections flash out simultaneously but the cameras in common use employed screens between the crystal and the film that only allowed spots lying on straight lines to be recorded on the film. The existing types of microdensitometers could then measure these spots, one line at a time.

With the availability of our computer-controlled device we could dispense with the screens and record and measure all the reflections that occurred. I encouraged my research student, Paul Phizackerley, to explore the technique that became known as the 'screen-less oscillation method'. Alan Wonacott and others in our laboratory and elsewhere developed computer programs to locate and measure the X-ray reflections. After we had published a description of the precision version of the rotation camera, which we had designed and which was built in our instrument workshop, the Dutch company Enraf-Nonius approached us and acquired a licence from the MRC and manufactured the camera.

We were very impressed by the efficiency with which the commercial version was developed. After they had studied the complete drawings of our instrument, two Dutch engineers came to Cambridge, one a mechanical and one an electronic engineer, each with a long list of highly detailed questions. When we had answered them all, I asked what the next step would be. 'We shall go back to Delft and build the instrument,' was the answer, and they did.

I shall always regret a sin of omission. At a laboratory seminar I announced that, for a given angle of oscillation, a crystal of a substance with small molecules gave rise to few X-ray reflections, so it was more efficient to measure these with a single radiation detector, one at a time. However, a crystal of a large-molecular material produced so many reflections per unit angle of oscillation that it was more efficient to record them on film, using the screen-less oscillation method. Without a question from Francis Crick as to where the crossover point in molecular size came, I would probably never have worked it out or written what turned out to be a fairly important paper, in which I failed to record my indebtedness to Francis's question. So, twenty years later, here is my declaration of *mea culpa*.

So useful was our computer-linked microdensitometer that we produced another one, which was slower but could cope with a larger range of photographic densities and this was followed by several other instruments, some for X-ray films and some for electron microscope photographs. The series, and also the Enraf-Nonius oscillation camera, only came to an end when photographic X-ray film was replaced by the Japanese Image Plate, which can be exposed, scanned, erased and reused many times. The method of use and the software of today's Image Plate X-ray cameras are the direct descendants of our screen-less oscillation technique.

In a way the success of the oscillation camera was an unexpected one. At the outset I had thought of it only as providing a method of testing the idea photographically before proceeding to the real instrument, which would record diffraction patterns by means of a purely electronic X-ray detector, such as a television camera. This real instrument was to occupy me on and off until my retirement.

The design and construction of apparatus and the development of new methods and techniques kept me completely happy and satisfied. I have frequently had visits from former colleagues and other scientific friends who have told me how lucky I was still to be working at the bench, and how they would like to do the same but were prevented by their duties on the faculty committee or the college wine committee, the executive committee of the inter-national union or the need to organise workshops or summer schools, by their editorial duties and by the need to attend several scientific meetings every year.

Invitations to all these activities are flattering and hard to resist: we all enjoy being consulted as experts, but one must remember the definition of a consultant expert given by my tutor, Edward Welbourne, as someone who has convinced other people to pay him for understanding a language that he has invented himself. A member of the planning committee for a new labora-tory or a new central facility, such as a major new radiation source, often reaches retirement age by the time that the laboratory or facility opens its doors. One of my heroes is Fred Sanger who always met invitations to sit on organising committees, editorial boards, and the like with the response that he was not very good at that sort of thing and that they should find someone else who would be much better at it than he. Fred went on working at the bench and won a second Nobel Prize, one of only three scientists to do so.

Part of the reason for my contentment with my situation was no doubt due to the fact that, at that period, scientists were comparatively well off compared with other professions. In addition to educating our daughters privately, we could afford to go on a two-week skiing holiday most winters and on a walking holiday of the same length in the Lake District most summers.

Our favourite hotel there was the Bridge Hotel at Buttermere, which was owned by a delightful couple, the Twitchins, who ran the hotel like a club. Many guests came year after year – we went nine times – and one could always count on meeting old acquaintances there. Newcomers were never booked in for more than four nights. If they did not prove their worth, they found the next year that, unfortunately, there was no room free until the end of November. Rodney Twitchin waged a long battle against the less choosy Fish Hotel next door. During our first stay, Elizabeth, then seven years old, announced in the bar: 'I have been thinking about the Fish.' Electrified silence, then: 'Yes, I think it's more of a teenagers' hotel.' We were on the list of approved guests!

In 1967, our third daughter, Annabel, was born. The two older ones, Elizabeth and Caroline, were leading very busy lives, what with school, ballet classes and swimming lessons all in Cambridge. We acquired a Mini as a second car to help our Rover deal with the ferrying runs. It was Valerie who foresaw that the dice would be loaded against driving and we started to look for a house near the centre of Cambridge, particularly a house that lent itself to having a granny flat built on for my mother whose health was deteriorating.

In her seventies, she had contracted tuberculosis from an old lady whom she was nursing. After a miserable period in and out of hospitals, she seemed to be improving when she died suddenly while on a visit to Cambridge. She never saw the house in Barrow Road, for which we had made an offer and where we had planned the flat for her that was never built. I am glad that, in the last two years of what had been a hard life, she derived so much pleasure from the company of her granddaughters. I owe a tremendous amount to her and I hope that I made her life a little easier and happier in the years after my father's death.

We had bought our house in Little Shelford with the help of a private mortgage from my mother. When she died just before I exchanged contracts on the new house in Barrow Road, I had to get a bridging loan from the bank until probate was granted, thus providing the sort of situation about which bank managers dream, in that the bank was getting interest on the loan to me of what amounted to my own money.

We quickly discovered the advantages of living in Barrow Road, with its line of flowering cherry trees, one of the most attractive roads in Cambridge. I now took only twelve minutes by bicycle to get to the MRC laboratory and I hardly ever needed a car. (Thirty years later, thanks to an electrically-assisted bicycle, it still takes me less than a quarter of an hour. In the meantime a car park has been allocated to our lab at the far edge of the Addenbrooke's Hospital site, which is a brisk twelve minutes' walk away from my office, so I am still quicker by bike.)

There were several children in Barrow Road going to the same schools as our girls so it was easy to join in a car pool. Later, when the girls were at the Perse School for Girls, they cycled there by themselves. Extra activities, such as Caroline's ballet classes, were much easier to arrange than they were from Shelford. According to a taxi driver Barrow Road was famous as the only road in England containing two inhabitants (George Steiner and Sir Roy Calne), who had appeared on Desert Island Discs on the radio. There was a pleasant and congenial social life among our neighbours. One of the Barrow Road traditions was the Boxing Day walk across the fields to Nine Wells, followed by tea at the house of David and Diana Kendall and their six children. The Kendall Walk generally attracted twenty to thirty people.

Our next door neighbours turned out to be Robert (Bobby) Gardner, a former bursar of Emmanuel, and his delightful wife. Thanks largely to Bobby, I was invited to dine regularly on Emmanuel High Table, which I greatly enjoyed for many years, until my contemporaries gradually retired or died off.

High Table conversation is a bit of a lottery: one may have an interesting and pleasant neighbour or one may be landed with someone who kills any attempt at a conversation. The story is told of a guest on St John's College High Table who attempted, with zero success, to get a response out of Professor PAM Dirac, the great theoretical physicist, until finally he asked in desperation: 'Have you read any good books recently?'

He was asked in turn: 'Why do you want to know?'

I once had a question which arose out of something I had read about the First Crusade, that I put to my neighbour who had told me that he was a mediaeval historian. He said, rather chillingly,

'That happened in the second half of the twelfth century; I specialise in the first half!'

We once took Valerie's South African cousin, Howard Stockdale, to a drinks party in Barrow Road. He said that he would not know how to talk to all these academic types. I told him that whoever he was introduced to would ask him: 'What is your subject?' and then, without waiting for a reply, would tell him what his own subject was. To my delight, that is exactly what happened, not once but twice.

In 1971 I had the good fortune to be present at the start of an important new scientific development. It had become apparent that some of the higher voltage electron synchrotrons that had been, or were being, built for nuclear physics experiments could be used as powerful sources of X-rays in the wavelength range of interest to crystallography. Ken Holmes, with his co-workers, Gerd Rosenbaum and Jean Witz, from Heidelberg, had built a beam-line to exploit the synchrotron radiation (SR), from a port of the new German electron synchrotron (DESY) in Hamburg and I had gone there to assist them in getting what was to be the first SR photograph of a muscle specimen.

We took all day to get everything ready for the moment when the beam was switched on for the evening shift. Ken Holmes had a gentleman's agreement with his former colleague Hugh Huxley, who had developed the mirrors and monochromators and the techniques for examining muscles, that frog sartorius muscle belonged to Hugh; Ken could concentrate on insect flight muscle. (Such gentleman's agreements were common in the early days, when it was not done to start a structure determination on which someone else was known to be working.) Accordingly, Holmes and his team brought along a specimen of a water beetle flight muscle, which had not been photographed properly before on a conventional X-ray source. With some effort, Ken was persuaded that it would be valuable to get one photograph of a well known material in order to make quantitative comparisons of the two sources.

As evening fell, Gerd Rosenbaum was dispatched to go frog hunting at a neighbouring pond in the company of the son of the

DESY porter. They failed to catch a frog, but, luckily, the muscle photograph turned out to be sufficiently good to make a powerful case for the continued development of SR sources at DESY and elsewhere.

The original synchrotrons at DESY and at Palo Alto in California were built for nuclear physics experiments. The X-ray work by Ken and his co-workers and by Keith Hodgson and his group from Stanford was parasitic to the nuclear physicists' work, for which the synchrotrons had been designed.

Later, the production of SR became the tail that wagged the dog: existing synchrotrons were converted into storage rings and new storage rings were built specifically as SR sources, mostly with a large number of beam-lines so that many simultaneous users could be accommodated.

Crystallography had now entered the big machine age. Crystal structure work was no longer a cheap field that could be pursued by small groups of researchers with relatively inexpensive apparatus. Everyone was now clamouring for access to large centralised facilities that were shared between dozens and later hundreds of users. And, what these centres needed more than anything else was a plethora of committees. Committees to plan the building of new synchrotrons, committees to screen and schedule access to beam-time, committees to consider the safety aspects of working with these powerful sources of radiation, and committees to plan the refurbishing and modernising of existing sources. It was difficult not to be drawn into the vortex. The larger European committees had American participants who, amongst other things, had to make sure that the Americans were keeping up with the Europeans. The larger American committees had European members who saw to it that the Europeans kept up with the Americans. As a result, the same people met on both sides of the Atlantic, merely changing hats as they crossed the ocean. By 2005 there were synchrotron radiation sources in more than twenty-five countries and the X-ray flux at the most intense beam lines was fourteen orders of magnitude greater than that at the most powerful conventional X-ray tubes.

Soon many protein crystallographers thought little of making several multi-thousand mile trips a year to collect diffraction data at any centre where they could find a suitable beam-line. More importantly, funding agencies were prepared to finance such trips. Data collection runs were carried out in as many hours as the number of weeks necessary in earlier days.

The development of these shared resources accelerated the internationalisation of what had always been a field in which one's collaborators came from many different countries. One of the privileges of having worked in the field of molecular biology was that one had close colleagues and friends all over the world.

The demand for access to synchrotrons sources reinforced the case for setting up the European Molecular Biology Laboratory (EMBL) which, like CERN (Centre Européen pour la Recherche Nucléaire), would be able to undertake researches too expensive for individual national laboratories. John Kendrew, the chief advocate for setting up EMBL, had had to meet the criticism that there was really nothing sufficiently expensive in molecular biology to justify an international laboratory. The high-cost SR work came at the right moment and EMBL was planned at the outset with a main laboratory at Heidelberg and an outstation at DESY in Hamburg.

Another EMBL outstation was built at Grenoble, France, adjacent to the Institut Laue Langevin (ILL), to benefit from collaborative biological structure work with neutrons at the latter institute. The existence of the administrative machinery, at the tri-national (French, German and British) ILL, was one of the reasons adduced for building the European Synchrotron Radiation Facility (ESRF) next door to the ILL, instead of in Strasbourg, which would have been the location preferred by many French scientists. The decision led to considerable, but unsuccessful, agitation in Alsace, with car stickers and posters protesting against the 'betrayal' of Alsace, and its capital Strasbourg, by depriving them of the synchrotron.

The ILL was originally a joint Franco-German institution. It was founded as a result of the desire of General de Gaulle and President Adenauer to demonstrate the friendship of the two countries by a really expensive joint scientific endeavour. The construction of a laboratory built around a high-flux neutron beam reactor satisfied the requirements of being expensive, but neither France nor Germany had particularly strong schools of neutron beam research. The first director of the ILL, Heinz Meyer-Leibnitz, asked John Kendrew to find someone from Britain to come to Grenoble and to institute research projects, preferably in molecular biology. John Kendrew, in turn, persuaded me to explore the possibilities of going to the ILL.

After a visit of several days, during which I was received with great friendliness and hospitality, I came to the reluctant conclusion that I was the wrong person for the job. Meyer-Leibnitz and his French co-director, Bernard Jacrot, had built up a talented team of instrument designers and electronic and computer engineers, that is, of people in the field that I had made my own. What they were short of were scientists with a burning desire to solve a particular problem, preferably a biological problem, but who needed the local technical expertise and help to set up the experiments. I also felt that neutrons would be more useful in solid-state physics, in materials science, and in the study of magnetic materials than in biology. The more I argued these points, the more Meyer-Leibnitz and Jacrot said that they wanted me. Since Valerie and I loved France and the French and would enjoy the close proximity to skiing and mountain-walking areas, I allowed myself to be persuaded and agreed to come for a trial period of one year in the first instance.

To quite an extent, my misgivings turned out to be justified. I could never quite persuade myself that a large effort should be devoted to neutron beams if your prime interests were in biology. Also, the situation at the ILL changed drastically during the year I was there, in that the British Science Research Council (SRC) joined the institute as the third partner. Very definitely, it was the SRC, and not British science as a whole, that joined. The SRC was not interested in biological structures or in biological materials: those subjects belonged to the MRC who, quite correctly in my view, gave a lower priority to neutron studies. A group of British physicists who were supported by the SRC had more ideas of what they wanted to do with neutrons than had the French and Germans. The purpose of my presence in Grenoble was therefore disappearing. Nevertheless, I got quite a lot done during my time at the ILL. I started to design a radiation detector based on a television camera and much of the electronic circuitry for the detector was the same for neutron and X-ray applications. The neutron version never came to very much, but the one for X-rays was completed in Cambridge and later went into commercial production, once again by Enraf-Nonius in Delft.

The ILL was an interesting and successful attempt at Franco-German bridge-building. Meyer-Leibnitz once said to me, 'If someone complains to me that "that stupid man who has borrowed my oscilloscope has wrecked it", I know that we have succeeded, but if he says, "that stupid Frenchman", or, "that silly German", we will have failed.'

The address of the institute was 'Place de la Résistance, Avenue des Martyrs' and periodic commemoration ceremonies were held at the Martyrs' memorial, just outside the gates of the institute, Grenoble having been one of the centres of resistance against the occupying German forces during the War. Yet I never heard of a single case of xenophobic friction, either in the laboratory or in the town as the Germans drove past with their German car number plates.

It was amusing to see the different national characteristics. In France, the engineer is often held in higher esteem than the physicist, but the French engineers tend to be more theoretical and less pragmatic. In exact contrast to what I had expected in a laboratory with several occupants, the French tended to work in complete silence while the Germans talked, whistled and cracked jokes while working.

The great phrases in France are *'en principe'* and *'en pratique'*; in principle something is forbidden, but in practice everyone does it or, in principle there are no rules against it but in practice it is much better not to do it. I once looked for someone in his office and was told by his secretary that in principle he was there, but in practice she did not have the faintest idea where he was to be found.

The constant switching of languages was quite tiring. At that time, French and German were equally in common use, English being employed mainly for communication with other nationalities. I once came home to our flat and started to tell Valerie something of the day's happenings, when she interrupted me to say that she did not understand what I was saying. I repeated myself with no better results. Finally, she said that, while she spoke French, she did not know much German and that our normal language was English. I would have regarded such behaviour as utter affectation before I had experienced the Tower of Babel that was the ILL, but I was by then quite unaware of what language I had switched into.

The arrival of the British, after I had left Grenoble, changed things. English has largely displaced the other languages as a common medium. People who had previously addressed each other as '*Monsieur X*' and '*vous*', or '*Herr Y*' and '*Sie*', were now quite happy to call each other by their first names. I had sat in on many discussions with SRC delegations who were there to settle matters ranging from schools for children of visiting staff to the composition of internal committees. (The rule seemed to be that there must be representatives from all three member nations on every committee but that the chairman should not be too fluent in the other languages.)

I am afraid that the British negotiators were usually out-manoeuvred by the more professional French and German civil servants. Our people did not seem to realise the importance of not losing face and yielded when they should have been firm and were stubborn where they could have given in. There had been much speculation about the name of which British scientist would be added to Laue and Langevin to express British membership. It was a mistake when the SRC representatives said: 'Oh, it does not matter, it has always been that way; much better to leave it at that.' I have often wondered whether I was witnessing an example of sources of friction within the European Union.

With one exception, our family and domestic arrangements were more than adequate. The institute had bought and fully furnished a very pleasant first-floor flat with three bedrooms within easy walking distance from the *Lycée* to which Elizabeth and Caroline, then aged thirteen and twelve, went, and about fifteen minutes by car from the laboratory. As is common in France, but unfortunately not in England, we were within walking distance of the baker, a small grocery, and an excellent fruit and vegetable shop.

The snag was that we had no telephone and this remained so

during our stay. The French telephone system at that time was catastrophic. The waiting time for a phone was fifteen months and calls abroad, whether from the lab or from friends' telephones, at times took up to three hours to connect. When there was something urgent to discuss, it was simplest to send a telex to Cambridge asking them to phone at some pre-arranged time. The lack of a phone in the flat drove Valerie to despair. There were often unexpected visits in the lab from old friends from England whom I wanted to bring home for a meal and there was no way of letting Valerie know. On one occasion, which I have never been allowed to forget, the visitors were rather important and they got the girls' dinner, who, themselves, had to make do with sandwiches.

Valerie's other source of disappointment was that she never had more than an hour or so free at a time. She had hoped to go to lectures at the university, or to other cultural events, but our daughters' irregular school hours made that impossible. Grenoble had grown explosively from 30,000 to 300,000 inhabitants after the war. Schools were stretched to the limit and had to operate a shift system of lessons. During free periods pupils were not allowed on the school premises. School meals were not provided for pupils living nearby and whose mothers were not working.

Elizabeth and Caroline had gained an adequate knowledge of French at school in England, reinforced by staying with a French family for some weeks before school started, so they could manage. For a few weeks Caroline had special dispensation at school to write her history homework in the present tense because she had not yet learnt the past tense of French verbs. After three months both sisters were able to work on equal terms with their French classmates. Elizabeth struck a particularly beneficial bargain with a group of tough boys: they would look after her on the ski slopes and take her down the more difficult runs in return for her help with their English homework. At the end of the year they both had excellent school reports and were passed for promotion to the next class. (In French schools quite a large proportion were kept down and had to repeat the year.)

The member of the family who had the hardest time in France was Annabel, who was just five when we arrived. Friends had advised us to send her to a private *Ecole Maternelle* instead of the much larger state-run school. Unfortunately, she landed in a much harsher environment than the one in which she had been in Cambridge, an environment that Valerie always described as 'plasticine and discipline'. The teacher was very strict and there was very little teaching. Annabel was the only one who could read, though not, of course, in French. In retrospect, I realise we had not made it sufficiently clear to her that in France everyone would be speaking French and that it would take quite a while before she would be able to understand and converse.

When we took her away and sent her to a somewhat more congenial school, things went a little better. By the time we left she could speak French fluently with a perfect accent but when we returned to Cambridge, she fell into the hands of a not very sympathetic and not very competent teacher who tried to force an appalling English pronunciation on her. Thereafter, she took a dislike to French at school and she did not do well at it. Surprisingly, after she left school she did a business course in college that involved a placement job in France; her knowledge of the French language and her perfect accent re-emerged from her subconscious and she loved her time in Paris.

The other two girls also found it quite difficult to settle back into school in Cambridge. Perhaps they had grown away from their friends and perhaps they were treated rather unimaginatively by the school staff, who did not appreciate that the syllabus in France is very different from that in England, especially in science and mathematics.

I came away from Grenoble with a new respect for my many colleagues who had managed to transplant their families smoothly to a foreign country. We started with the advantage that neither Valerie nor I had any language problems and our daughters seemed to have natural linguistic abilities. We had been found pleasant accommodation and we all enjoyed the outdoor activities in Grenoble, the walking in the Vercors in summer and autumn, and the skiing in winter.

Even so, we found life much more of a strain on the nerves than at home. Valuable in keeping things going in England though they were, my flying visits to the lab in Cambridge about once a month were tiring. The vagaries of French bureaucracy were not always easy to understand. Some of my French colleagues had told me that I need not really bother to fill in an income tax return, since I would have left France before anyone had noticed that the form was missing. I did not want to play that game, but as a result of the arguments and because of a trip to England, I missed the deadline for sending in the form. That, apparently, was a heinous crime which could entail a heavy fine. However the nice man in the ILL personnel department, known to everyone as Monsieur Fixit, drafted me a letter of apology so creeping and self-abasing that I was almost sick when copying it out. Because I was only an ignorant Anglo-Saxon, not yet fully conversant with all the magnificent traditions of the glorious republic, on whose behalf I had just undertaken a mission abroad, I had committed an error for which I craved forgiveness from the generous-natured holder of the prestigious office of income tax inspector, etc. etc. It worked, for I heard no more on the subject.

It was most interesting to have been able to compare working practices in France and England. Two concepts, commonplace in British laboratories, did not appear to have crossed the Channel. They were Equality and Fraternity. There were rigid class distinctions between *'Cadres'* and 'non-*Cadres*', that is between those with high qualifications, especially qualifications from a *'grande école'*, and others who were merely university graduates. There were differences in types of handshakes and in the mode of address used between the classes of employees. The use of *'monsieur'* and *'madame'*, instead of first names, is not totally without significance. The professionalism of French engineering was very obvious, compared with a cheerful amateurism not uncommon in Britain. Full engineering drawings of every component of every instrument meant that much of the construction work would be farmed out to local manufacturers with high speed and efficiency. On the other hand, it was quite difficult to wander into the machine shop and to induce a machinist to drill another hole in the base-plate 'about there'. Unless, of course, one had first discovered which football team said machinist supported. So, perhaps, sometimes the differences were not as great as they appeared at first sight.

During the course of my research career, I have worked for

longer or shorter periods at several large national and inter-national laboratories: Harwell, the ILL, Brookhaven National Laboratory on Long Island in the States, the European Molecular Biology Laboratory in Heidelberg, and a few others. For big projects, such big institutes may be the most efficient or, indeed, the only possible places but, on the whole, I have found that I preferred working in smaller establishments.

LMB, Cambridge and round the world, 1973–1988

On my return to Cambridge from Grenoble, I went on working in the field of X-ray detectors which, like photographic film, could be used to measure how much X-ray intensity arrived at each point of a large area. These devices became known, somewhat misleadingly, as 'area detectors', and there was fierce rivalry between the advocates of the different types of such things. There were devices based on television cameras of various kinds and on semiconductors and detectors that relied on the absorption of X-ray in a gas layer. The development work was expensive and the expense led to the competitiveness in the field.

The rate of progress was also slow: in 1986 I wrote a review article in which I discussed the various detectors and described other innovations as being just around the corner. Twenty years later these were still just around the corner, but the corner was, perhaps, a little nearer. It is one of the vexations of doing research in a field involving new technology that one can often see years ahead highly useful and technically perfectly feasible advances. If these compete with commercially more profitable projects, one may have to wait a long time for progress. It was the tragedy of Walter Hoppe, a Munich professor of physics, that he had many excellent ideas in the fields of X-ray diffraction and electron microscopy for which the time was not yet ripe because simple technological solutions were still lacking. At meetings he would jump up after every paper, saying: 'in my laboratory we already this have done in 1951.' He could not understand the laughter which greeted his announcement that he had done something or other in 1984, a year then still far in the Orwellian future.

By 1975, a lot of interest had been created in the rotation method of taking X-ray photographs of protein crystals. Enraf Nonius had sold quite a few of the cameras that they were manufacturing to our design under the licence from the MRC. Software had been written in Cambridge, England, in Cambridge, Massachusetts, and in Munich, in what had been Hoppe's laboratory.

It was obviously desirable to share the experience gained in different places, to coordinate software developments, and to train new converts to the method. Accordingly, with the support of Enraf-Nonius we organised an international school in Groningen in the Netherlands. The school was appreciated by the participants and, at the end, there was a general feeling that the lecture notes should be expanded and given a more permanent form. Alan Wonacott and I agreed to act as editors of a monograph with sixteen contributors from nine different laboratories. In the end, Alan and I finished up by writing about seventy percent of the book ourselves. Several times a manuscript arrived long after the deadline when we had already just written up a particular subject ourselves in desperation. However, it was quite fun and I think the book has been useful. The process has certainly given me a profound respect for the heroes who voluntarily undertake similar editing tasks more than once.

During these years I was busy developing the prototype of our 'area detector'. Later I was a consultant during the production of the commercial version, which was also built under licence from the MRC by Enraf Nonius in Delft. The development of the instrument and indeed of area detector diffractometry in general owed much to David Thomas, who had joined me as a research student. Unfortunately, there was some friction between him and a Dutch engineer who did not always appreciate David's ability. I myself very much enjoyed my collaboration with the Dutch engineers and my frequent visits to Holland. These were especially interesting before there was a direct train connection from Delft to Schiphol Airport. In those days, I always tried to arrange my homeward journey so as to have an hour in the Mauritshuis in The Hague, my favourite picture gallery, before catching the airport bus. When the Schiphol railway station was opened, I lost that particular pleasure, but the journey from Cambridge to Delft became incredibly quick, especially while there was a direct air service between Cambridge and Amsterdam: my record time between closing the garage door at home and entering the Delft factory was two hours and forty minutes. My only regret is that I never started these journeys by cycling to Cambridge airport.

The development of the new diffractometer seemed painfully slow: we were working at the frontiers of technology and some of the devices we needed, especially computer peripherals, were slow to arrive on the market or they were still unreasonably expensive. At the core of our instrument was the image store, which held 135,000 bytes of information and which was driven by a large and expensive power supply. (In 2005, a modest portable computer had a store 2000 times larger.)

Valerie frequently pointed out to me that I was often off to exotic places in which she had no particular interest, but that if ever I had an invitation to South Africa she would come like a shot to spend some time with her favourite aunt, who was married to a farmer in the Orange Free State. Then one day I was asked, somewhat diffidently, whether I was ever likely to be interested in coming to South Africa, fares and expenses paid, and in giving lectures at several South African universities. I accepted on the spot without asking what sort of lectures or where and, in the spring of 1979, we set off by South African Airways. In those days of apartheid, other African states would not allow SAA planes to overfly their territories, let alone to land, and there was a large detour to the west for a refuelling stop in the Cape Verde Islands. At Jan Smuts Airport, the only place where I have ever had my luggage closely examined for forbidden pornographic literature, Valerie and I parted company, she to fly on to Bloemfontein and I to start my lecture tour, travelling to Pretoria, Johannesburg, Durban, East London, and Cape Town.

I found the Republic of South Africa a land of surprises. I had expected to see signs of racial tension between black and white, but saw equal tension between Indians and other races, and between darker-skinned and lighter-skinned Indians. I had been led to believe that English-speaking South Africans were on the side of the angels but that all Afrikaners were apostles of apartheid. I met instead a number of English-speakers who were loud in protesting their own liberalism and in condemning all Afrikaners for their racial intolerance and who then turned to a black maid or waiter and spoke to them with a cold lack of humanity. On the other hand, there was an Afrikaans-speaking scientist, who had been represented to me as a violent racist, who sent his children to a mixed-race school and who, at some danger to himself, had accommodated a relative of his black cook's in a room above his garage to save him from being sent to a township.

It is easy to succumb to prejudices oneself. In Durban, it was easier to feel sorry for the neat Indian children in their school blazers and white starched dresses than for the ragamuffin Zulu boys, both races equally banned from the 'whites only' beaches. Racial relations seemed much easier in Cape Town than in Durban or Johannesburg.

I had expected South African laboratories to be backward in computing, in view of the American ban on the export or re-export of computers to South Africa. In fact, American computers had found their way to South Africa quite freely.

But pre-eminent of all my impressions was the warm hospitality and friendliness shown to me. Everywhere I went I was entertained with great kindness and shown the local sites. At the end of my lecture tour I was treated to a marvellous three days in the Kruger National Park, before I joined Valerie in the Orange Free State for a few days. It was wonderful to be able to enjoy the clean air and the solitude in the High Veld. The Stockdales, Valerie's uncle and cousin, employed about a hundred people on the farm that could have been run with a far smaller number. They kept 'their people' on the books as, otherwise, they would have been forced into a shanty town.

In a conversation at the next farm about a problem which had arisen among the Stockdales' workforce, a neighbour commented that it was a pity that there was no witch doctor among their people who could have dealt with the problem easily. We visited the school set up by the Stockdales for the farm labourers' children. A head teacher and one assistant looked after the class of about thirty Basuto children. The head teacher was working for his English school certificate; he was a Zulu and it was very much to his credit that he got on well with his pupils and their families: normally, relations between Zulus and the Basutos are strained. We were asked to talk to the children about our girls' school in England. One lad wanted to know if there were any black children in their school and, when I told him that there were two, he wanted to know why there were not more. He obviously found it difficult to grasp that, in England, black people were a relatively small minority (this was in 1979). I noticed that the school had no form of artificial lighting: this was clearly unnecessary as throughout the year days are long enough for all school lessons to be fitted into daylight hours.

Unfortunately, the Stockdales had to leave the farm, which had been in their family for 120 years, not so long after our visit. The climate was becoming drier and the edges of the Kalahari Desert were moving south so it was becoming uneconomical to grow mixed crops.

We saw the need for water management on a day excursion to nearby Lesotho, an independent mountainous land-locked kingdom (the former Basutoland Protectorate). On the Orange Free State side of the frontier, all fields had been contour-ploughed and there was no obvious sign of erosion. In the Kingdom of Lesotho, the thin layer of topsoil was being washed away and the trees that had been planted in the Protectorate days were being felled.

Two years later, Valerie came with me to the United States, where I was due at a conference at the University of Virginia. This was Valerie's first visit to America. Having her with me, I saw more tourist sights than on most of my normal business trips. We made a tour of the New York museums, took a tourist bus round Manhattan, and the ferry to the Statue of Liberty. I was struck by how much more Spanish one now heard everywhere and by the sight of bicycles and skateboards in Manhattan.

We had taken advantage of the 'see America' scheme, under which there was a fifty percent discount on internal flights booked with one's transatlantic tickets. To save trouble later, I confirmed our onward flight to Washington on arrival at Kennedy airport. The clerk at the BA counter looked at our tickets. 'Gee, you guys have been robbed in London,' he said. 'A New York to Washington ticket should not cost you more than half the discounted price you paid. Here, I will cancel these sections and get you tickets from a small airline and you can get refunds when you get back home.' Without giving us a chance to think, he cancelled our tickets and continued: 'Coming to think of it, you have a more comfortable and more interesting journey, which is just as quick, if you travel by Amtrak.'

So at the end of our time in New York we went to Pennsylvania railroad station were Valerie got our tickets at the counter while I dealt with our luggage. The clerk said to her: 'Are you guys married?'

Valerie was just about to reply: 'What has that to do with you?' when he went on. 'Special offer this weekend for married couples: two for the price of one.' And indeed, we did get our plane tickets refunded when we got back home! On the train we got involved in a lively discussion about the American Civil War, known to Americans as the War between the States. One of the men sitting opposite us was a black railroad engineer, the other a white professor from the Georgia Institute of Technology. Another sign of change in the States: I did not think that such a conversation would have taken place when I first visited the US, twenty years earlier. By the time we reached Princeton, several other people had joined in the discussion, making it one of my most interesting train journeys.

In Washington we enjoyed ourselves doing all the things one ought to do. Over lunch in the cafeteria of the National Gallery of Art a couple sitting at the same table asked us whether we were English and then: 'How does it feel to be at war?' making us guess who we were at war with. It was the beginning of the Falklands campaign and we certainly would not have guessed.

From Washington we moved on to the University of Virginia at Charlotte, where we were put into a beautiful eighteenth century guest room for a meeting of the American Crystallographic Association. I met a lot of old friends and I had to stand in for a Nobel laureate, Bill Lipscomb of Harvard, who had had to cancel his attendance and in whose stead I was asked to make the after dinner speech in the beautiful rotunda designed by Thomas Jefferson.

1982 was an amazing year for me, in which I was elected a Fellow of the Royal Society. Unexpectedly for me, I had been proposed nearly five years before and, by now, I was certain that I had failed to be elected. Being on the list of candidates is a strange situation. I knew that all existing fellows see the list – one or two had written to wish me luck and to warn me that election was far from assured. In fact, only about one third of those proposed are elected. In March, the forty successful candidates are informed and congratulations arrive from existing fellows to whom the list is communicated. The news remains strictly confidential for about four weeks and then it is announced in the press, after which one receives congratulations from others. Those letters are among the nicest things about the election. After the admission ceremony the new fellows sign the Register of Fellows with a quill pen. The book is still the one that has the signature of Charles II on the first page and then those of Newton, Boyle, Pepys, and all the others on subsequent pages. It is all very impressive and also rather awe-inspiring. At the lunch for new fellows, before the ceremony, I said that I was certain that I was the most ignorant person ever to be elected to the august body, and was glad to hear that sentiment echoed all round the table.

One of the results of being entitled to put the letters FRS after one's name is that one is entitled to be included in *Who's Who*. My accountant started to address me as 'professor', as did the inspector of taxes. When I told my accountant that I was not in fact a professor he advised me not to tell the Inland Revenue, who knew that professors might be forgetful and absent-minded but were rarely outright dishonest.

Among the guests in the hotel in Buttermere that year, where we were spending our customary Lake District holiday, were two other Fellows of the Royal Society. When two ladies who were just leaving the hotel came back from the car park announcing that they had a flat tyre, the three of us jumped up offering our help. On the way to the car the other two, who were biologists, claimed that matters concerning machinery were the province of physicists and not biologists and I was elected to change the tyre.

In the summer of 1983, Valerie and I celebrated our silver wedding anniversary with a garden party at home in perfect summer weather. The very next day I had to leave on a round-the-world journey. I was to teach at a summer school in Kyoto, Japan, and found it much easier to get funding for this trip if it was part of a study tour in Japan. I very much wanted to see how the Japanese scientific instrument industry was functioning, so the Japanese part of the journey grew into a fortnight. I had promised my friend Sandy Mathieson, in Melbourne that the next time I visited Japan, I would spend a little time in Australia. An appropriate number of days after I was due to leave Melbourne there was a meeting in Long Island, New York, so I decided to fly across the Pacific and to spend a couple of days in California before coming home via New York. My round the world ticket entitled me to spend one night each in Bangkok and Hong Kong without extra cost, and that is how my plans had grown.

I found Bangkok fascinating, Hong Kong fascinating (and unexpectedly beautiful), and my pre-summer school week in Japan exhausting. As on other visits there, I had the feeling that my feet were too big, my behaviour insufficiently courteous, and that my wishes as to what I wanted to see put my Japanese hosts to far too much trouble. I had incautiously expressed an interest in high-definition television in the hope that equipment developed for this purpose could lead to inexpensive improvements of our X-ray detector. I was promptly taken to a big department store on the Ginza in Tokyo where there was an exhibition of such television sets with 120 degree wraparound images of Cinemascope quality.

My visit to the factory of Rigaku-Denki, leading manufacturer of X-ray instruments, left me with an enormous stack of visiting cards and the discovery that Japanese businessmen carefully file and consult these cards: one of the engineers showed me a card of mine that he had annotated and which I had given to him at a conference ten years earlier. I was puzzled by the huge range of the company's X-ray products, most of which had never been seen in the West or been listed in Western catalogues. The answer to my question of how they could afford to make so many different instruments, any one of which would surely only be sold in small numbers, was, 'Computer-aided design and automated machinery'. I certainly saw more signs of automation than in a western factory producing scientific instruments. However, I believe that the main explanation was that MITI, the Ministry of International Trade and Industry, paid for the construction of a new instrument, which was then loaned or given to a university for careful evaluation and only products that received favourable reports ever appeared on the international market.

At the Fuji factory, which I also visited, I utterly failed to recognise the potential of a prototype X-ray sensitive image plate, which has since revolutionised X-ray radiography and crystallography by very largely replacing X-ray films. Obviously, I would not have been a very successful industrial spy.

The summer school in Kyoto, the main reason for my journey, had students from all over eastern Asia, including China, Taiwan, Thailand, Malaysia, India, and Korea. It was very noticeable that all of these were much more forthcoming in asking the lecturers questions and in joining in discussions than the native Japanese. We felt that the Japanese were afraid of a loss of face, their own, by showing that there was something that they had not understood, and the lecturers, who obviously had not made things sufficiently clear, if there was a need for questions.

I was met at Sydney airport by George Fisher, cousin of my old friend Tony Fisher, who, during the war, had spent a brief period at Emmanuel College in Cambridge. He and his wife received me most hospitably in their bungalow in an attractive suburb of Sydney, where I was cheered greatly by seeing a photograph of our cat that George had taken on a visit a year or so before.

In my hotel I found a leaflet advertising a special offer of an afternoon tour of the Opera House, followed by dinner in the restaurant there and a ticket for Strauss *Rosenkavalier*, which I booked by phone on the spot. I was much impressed by the Opera House in its beautiful setting. For dinner I found myself at a table with a cheery group of people, one of whom asked me what was my branch in physiology. When I said none, I was a crystallographer, they asked me what I was doing at the International Congress of Physiology, which they were all attending. Although I did not actually know any of my fellow diners, we had plenty of acquaintances in common. We met again during the interval of a very fine performance of the *Rosenkavalier*.

A few days later, I went with Sandy Mathieson to Newcastle, to the annual conference of the Australian Crystallographic Association, or the Bush Crystallographers, as they call themselves. One of the first people I met there was Hans Freeman, professor of crystallography in Sydney and an old acquaintance. He asked me if he had seen me at the Opera House a few days before. 'I did not want to disturb you; you were obviously with a large group of friends.'

The drive from Newcastle to Melbourne with Sandy and his wife, Lois, showed me a little of the Australian landscape, but the only kangaroo I saw was in a zoo in Melbourne. It rained most of the time I was there, but I had a most enjoyable time staying with the Mathiesons. Sandy is an Aberdonian who emigrated to Australia after getting his PhD at Glasgow. I have met him at many conferences and meetings and during some of his sabbatical visits to Britain and the USA. He is one of that small band of friends whom one sometimes does not see for years, but with whom one can resume a conversation at any time as though it had only been interrupted for an hour.

During these days, we had deep discussions about crystallography. We sketched out a joint research programme for which, unfortunately, neither of us could produce the experimental facilities. However, some of the ideas that I had then found their way into a *Festschrift* for Sandy when he retired from the CSIRO, (Commonwealth Scientific and Industrial Research Organisation) two years later.

I had thought that the long flight from Melbourne to San Francisco, with stops in Sydney, Hawaii and Los Angeles, would separate the men from the boys but, in fact, I found it little more taxing than the short hop across the Atlantic. However, I did fall gratefully into my bed in a motel room in Palo Alto where I had gone by limousine straight from the airport, only to be woken up by a loud voice just outside my window, saying over and over again, 'Now remove the ignition key, now remove the ignition key'. Fortunately, after half an hour the driver returned and did.

I knew that I had arrived in Silicon Valley the next morning. While I was having my breakfast in the coffee shop, I was observing what I took to be a truck driver and his wife and son as they tucked into an enormous stack of hot cakes. And I heard the boy say to his mother: 'No, Mum. With that percentage of indium, I guess you'll find that it'll crystallise in a monoclinic space group.'

I spent a pleasant day at Stanford with Paul Phizackerley, my former research student, now a full professor at Stanford, and then flew on to New York for my final scientific meeting of the journey at Brookhaven National Laboratory. By the time I got to New York, I felt that I was practically home.

During the next five years I continued to publish a series of papers on our X-ray television diffractometer, papers which now look suspiciously like *Television Diffractometer, More Television Diffractometers, Television Diffractometer Rides Again* and *Son of Television Diffractometer.* But I suppose the papers familiarised people with this and similar instruments and with the use of area detectors in general for collecting X-ray data on protein crystals and solving their structures. At any rate, I continued to receive invitations to give lectures and to attend various meetings and conferences. At one such conference in Hamburg, I had bought a ticket for a very modern production of the *Magic Flute* at the Opera House. As I sat down, a voice behind me asked whether I spent all my time at the Opera. It was Hans Freeman from Sydney and actually, for both of us, it was the first time that we had been to the opera since the Sydney *Rosenkavalier*.

As a result of other commitments, I could not join Valerie on a most exciting journey. Our daughter, Caroline, after qualifying as a doctor, spent a year at a missionary hospital in Lesotho in 1986 and, during some of this time, she was in sole charge of a branch hospital at Tebellong in the mountains, some fifty kilometres from the nearest town. Valerie visited her there, having hitched a ride from the Flying Doctor service. In the clear air they had the most superb views of Halley's comet. That year the Royal Society's soirée featured an exhibition of photographs of the comet taken by the expedition that had gone to Chile for observations. Valerie caused some consternation by pointing out that she had had a much clearer view of the bifurcation of the comet's tail than was visible on the official photographs.

Our lives were changing slowly. Elizabeth, now a qualified solicitor, married in 1987 and Caroline in 1988. Even Annabel, our youngest, had finished her course of business studies and was now in her first job. We gradually substituted walking in the Alps for our annual Lake District pilgrimages, having discovered the advantages of taking a cable car up and only having to walk down. I had damaged my right hip joint in a skiing accident many years earlier and the joint was becoming arthritic. I thought it would be easier to get a hip replacement operation done under the National Health Service while I was still in full employment. My official retirement was due in 1989 when I reached the age of sixty-five, and I was operated on in December 1988. Hip replacement and cataract operations (which I had some years later), spoil you for any other surgical intervention if they go well, which they did for me. You go into hospital with something seriously wrong and, a surprisingly short time later, you are as good as new.

Just before my operation, I spent a few rather uncomfortable days in Moscow. I had become interested in some Russian work on X-ray optics and keenly accepted the invitation to an international conference and exhibition that had been puffed up as a meeting at which foreign visitors could make contact with Russian colleagues. We were invited to supply a list of the laboratories that we wanted to visit and the scientists whom we wanted to meet and we were told we would have the opportunity of studying recent Russian achievements in scientific instrumentation. The meeting was the most disorganised one that I have ever attended. Of the four scientists I wanted to meet, two were reputed to be in Siberia and one in Paris, so I could not visit their institutes. The fourth gave me a very hurried tour of his laboratory and then took me out to a most sumptuous lunch in a very elegant restaurant where all the other guests seemed to be high ranking officers. After lunch, I expected to return to the laboratory but was instead taken on a sightseeing tour of Moscow – at a temperature of minus ten degrees Celsius. In the Academy of Sciences Hotel, where we were all put up in rather primitive but well-heated double rooms, sharing with total strangers, I met Pierre Dhez, a French visitor who had spent the previous four days with the two Russians who were supposedly in Siberia and I was fortunate in finding out from him most of what I had hoped to learn from the Russians.

The next day, I was taken to a pavilion in the huge exhibition ground. After walking round a little I noticed that all the instruments on show were from West Germany. 'Of course,' I was told, 'this is the German pavilion.'

At my request we made our way through the snow to the Russian pavilion, where I saw interesting equipment but nothing very different from Western instruments, with which I was familiar. The exhibitors seemed very keen to talk but, as it was just before closing time, there was not much of an opportunity.

The foreign visitors' lectures the following day were on a succession of totally unrelated subjects. In the afternoon, I met a Russian who told me that he had come from outside Moscow to hear my talk and who was dismayed to hear that I had spoken before lunch. At the beginning of the session we had been asked by the Russian chairman to stand in silence for one minute to honour the victims of Stalinist repression. *Glasnost* had arrived!

I have said above that it was one of the most disorganised meetings that I have ever attended. It was also the most puzzling and the most incomprehensible one. The high spot of the visit for me was an excursion with the senior professor and my 'nanny' to Zagorsk monastery, some thirty kilometres from Moscow. There was some discussion between the two Russians on whether I had a dispensation to go so far away from Moscow. We actually did something that was apparently quite illegal: we left the main road and made a detour to a little chapel standing all by itself in the middle of nowhere, surrounded by fields of undisturbed snow and with long icicles hanging from the roof. It is the view of that little church that will stay with me longer than any other Russian memory.

Three days after coming home, I went into hospital to have my hip replacement operation and, by Christmas, I was able to get about on crutches.

Retirement projects, 1989–2004

In 1989, I retired from my position on the MRC staff. I lost the large laboratory in which I had hoped to carry out experiments on the coherence of X-ray beams, but I also had plans to come back to some work on X-ray generation and on X-ray optics which were effectively a continuation of what I had done for my PhD thesis in 1948.

The MRC had a system called Retired Workers' Project Grants that could be held for three-year periods. These grants were intended, it was explained to me, for replacing the shoe leather worn out in walking to the lab. I was fortunate in getting two such consecutive grants and also a Royal Society Paul Instrument Fund grant for developing some new pieces of X-ray optics. The Russian ideas, as explained to me by Pierre Dhez in the seventh floor cafeteria of the Academy Hotel in Moscow, did not seem very practical for what I had in mind, but a literature search revealed that a group in Prague had produced some interesting X-ray mirrors, which were flown in Russian satellites as the key components of X-ray telescopes for observing X-ray-emitting stars. X-ray optics was then, and is still, something of a speciality in eastern bloc countries.

A letter to Czechoslovakia resulted in a number of Czech reprints, together with a rather charming letter asking why someone in a laboratory of molecular biology was interested in X-ray astronomy. I wrote back and explained my aim was to produce a well-focused X-ray beam from a small-diameter X-ray source for crystallographic studies. After some further correspondence, the Czechs offered to try to make the sort of mirrors that I had in mind, which were much smaller than what they had made so far. Under communism, it appeared relatively easy to get permission and funding for such projects and I was invited to go to Prague to discuss plans. Valerie, who had never been on the far side of the Iron Curtain, decided to come with me. While we were still making our preparations, the Berlin Wall fell in December 1989, followed swiftly by the Velvet Revolution in Czechoslovakia.

The euphoria and the optimism in Prague when we arrived there in June 1990 were very moving to experience. Walking across the Charles Bridge, our guide would stop and point at a group of students chatting together and say: 'Look, for years an assembly of more than five people would have been illegal.' Or in the Metro: 'There are three people in this coach reading newspapers. Under communism, we never read the papers because we knew that they contained only lies.' As the first Western visitors whom most of our Czech hosts had met, we were received with great warmth and hospitality and people vied with one another in showing us their beautiful city of which they were so justifiably proud. Strangers came up to us in the tram or in a Metro station and wanted to try out their meagre English or French on us. We were warned that too good a knowledge of English tended to betray a trusty communist, as others had not often been allowed to study English. People over sixty could usually be relied on to speak German.

I was astonished to see how obviously western Prague was. We were put up in the hotel of the Czech Academy of Sciences, which was vastly different from the shabby USSR Academy hotel in Moscow where I had been not so long before and where the staff had mostly been rather surly. There were, of course, still many signs of life under communism: restaurants had numbers rather than names, food was pretty monotonous and there were obvious shortages. We were told that these were mainly due to the need to feed the Russian troops who, wisely, were not in evidence and who were being withdrawn as quickly as possible. People were quite well and smartly dressed, though there was not a great deal in shop windows. A bookshop had a display of books by Kafka and other writers in pre-1939 editions; these had obviously been lying in a storeroom for fifty years.

The outward signs of communism were being removed. Near our hotel, a more than life-size statue of Stalin was being demolished and we saw the head being driven past on a lorry for the benefit of television cameras. At the foot of a television mast, we saw four large Soviet stars, which had been removed from the top of the mast. One evening we came back from the centre of

Prague by Metro after going to the opera. When we duly got out of the train at the fifth stop, we found a completely unfamiliar station name. Fortunately I spotted the place where the name we had seen that morning, of a Russian revolutionary hero, had been chiselled out during the day. The old station names were being restored all over Prague.

We went to the opera twice. *Il Seraglio*, on tickets obtained from the central tourist office, which had the atmosphere of a Russian *Intourist* office, and *The Marriage of Figaro*, which we had been told was sold out, on tickets bought, more cheaply, from a tout outside the opera house. Valerie spotted on both occasions that the soloists were taking their timing from the conductor instead of the other way round as is customary in non-totalitarian operas. In 2000, we again visited Prague and saw *Don Giovanni* in the opera house where Mozart had directed the premiere of that opera; the conductor now took his timing from the soloists.

On Sunday we were taken to Konopiste, a castle and hunting lodge, some thirty kilometres from Prague. As soon as we saw it, we both decided that it must have acted as the model for Anthony Hope's *Prisoner of Zenda*. It fitted the description so well that we expected Douglas Fairbanks to come galloping across the drawbridge.

In between all these activities, the Czechs and I managed to decide on a possible mirror design and to draw up a programme on some aspects of which we were still collaborating fifteen years later.

There were, of course, considerable problems to be overcome. The Czech physicists and engineers whom I met on this, and later, visits had many original ideas and had developed many experimental skills, but they were handicapped by a lack of modern automated machine tools and, above all, by a lack of computers. The money to make good these shortages had to be earned by engaging in profitable commercial ventures. Managerial and business skills were in short supply amongst all but a small number of managers who had been installed under the communists, and many of these had been compulsorily retired. Sometime later, I tried to clear up problems that had arisen when the Czechs had manufactured some expensive mirrors on an overseas customer's letter of enquiry. I discovered that they had interpreted the enquiry as an order and did not know the difference between a quotation and an invoice. After some time, the group of scientists from the Czech Technical University, the State Institute of Materials Sciences, and the Academy of Sciences Astronomical Institute, all of whom had been involved in the discussions, obtained a loan from the Czech government to set up a limited liability company. I felt a little guilty over what I had started when I asked one of them what his ambition was and got the answer: 'To live the life of a Western businessman.' And even guiltier ten years later when he had succeeded and, I suspected, did not like the life of a businessman nearly as much as he had expected.

Supported by my two successive grants from the MRC, I worked out, on paper, the outline design of a microfocus X-ray tube for use with the Czech type of mirror. A calculation showed that there was a possibility that such a combination could produce a higher intensity at a much lower electrical power than the much larger X-ray generators in normal use.

For many years, Valerie had been in the habit of meeting two friends for coffee once a week after the Arts Lectures for Physicists at the Cavendish Laboratory. When these lectures came to an end, Valerie, and the wives of Jim Long and Peter Duncumb, two specialists in electron optics and X-ray generation, whom I had known for a very long time, but with whom I had never worked, continued to meet regularly. Over coffee, Valerie told her friends of my ideas and they told their husbands. The result was that the three of us decided to collaborate in producing a microfocus X-ray tube to a much better design than I could ever have achieved by myself. In addition, Jim Long was able to offer me space in his laboratory next to a disused high voltage supply that we could use for the prototype tube once it was built.

We obtained the grant to build an X-ray tube from the Royal Society and, raiding the scrap heaps of both laboratories, we were able to construct our tube remarkably cheaply.

An old acquaintance of mine – and a friend of Peter Duncumb's – was Keith Bowen, now Professor of Material Sciences at Warwick University and part-time director of Bede

Scientific Instruments Ltd, a small company in Durham that manufactured a range of X-ray instruments. At Peter's suggestion, he and I visited Keith in Warwick for metallurgical advice on a problem that had arisen with the Czech mirrors. Keith was very interested in the design of our X-ray tube and eventually acquired a licence from the MRC for Bede to manufacture and market the tube. Bede also bought the limited liability company which my friends in Prague had set up and the Czech group became directors of the now wholly-owned subsidiary of Bede Ltd and thus they all became Western-style businessmen.

I had a fairly serious operation in 1993 and so refused offers of any directorships. As a result, I took no part in the decision to subcontract manufacture of the X-ray tube to Oxford Instruments, Inc, in Palo Alto, California. This contracting out made the tube rather expensive so it did not compete too well with other microfocus X-ray tubes that were now beginning to appear on the market.

In 1995, I got involved in an interesting, though never in my view scientifically very promising, project. In some early NASA experiments carried out on aeroplanes flown on vertical parabolic trajectories, weightlessness had been achieved for more than a minute. Material scientists had obtained better quality crystals from some substances when crystallised under these zero gravity conditions. Protein crystallographers, for whom crystal quality has always been a problem, obtained disappointing results when trying to crystallise proteins under these conditions.

'Ah,' said some, 'we did get better crystals but they were ruined on re-entry.'

'So,' said someone else at a committee meeting, 'we must plan to put an X-ray tube and an X-ray diffractometer into the planned International Orbiting Space Lab and carry out the complete operation of growing the crystals and determining their structure in space at zero gravity.'

From what I know of this second 'someone', the suggestion was possibly not an entirely serious one, although he has maintained to me that it was. At any rate, it was resolved to put such experiments on the programme of the International Space Lab and inquiries were made of all manufacturers of X-ray generators and diffractometers whether extra-light and extra-small versions of their instruments could be produced, but this was generally pronounced as impossible. Then someone at Princeton University, who was a consultant to NASA, heard of our microfocus tube and contacted me with an offer of financial support for a 'space' version of our instrumentation. I referred them to the Bede people, who became very enthusiastic and thought that it would be a splendid advertisement to have been the manufacturers of the first space X-ray laboratory.

I went to a couple of meetings at the University of Alabama in Birmingham and to a meeting in Huntsville, where I saw a splendid NASA movie on a wide Cinerama screen and met there a real live astronaut who gave me a signed photograph of himself in a space suit to pass on to my grandchildren. The children were very interested to know that the planes used for the parabolic zero gravity flights were universally known as the 'vomit comets' because the flights made everyone sick.

Bede sold a tube to the University of Alabama, where the terrestrial proving of the apparatus was to take place, and one of their best engineers spent far too much time in Birmingham to the detriment of scientifically more useful projects. I have seen photographs of remarkably compact prototype modules for the space station but, as far as I know, the project has died unsung and mostly unlamented.

Since the nineties I seem to have been involved in a technological game of leapfrog. During most of my research career, the standard X-ray source for crystallography, and especially for the crystallography of large biological molecules, has been the continuously-pumped rotating anode X-ray tube, and most of us have hated these dirty, noisy, and awkwardly large beasts. At best, instead of doing more profitable things, we have had to spend too much time on the maintenance and service of the brutes. At worst, we have ruined our clothes and shoes with vacuum pump oil or caught our hair in the belt drive of the rotating anode. In contrast, the micro-focus X-ray tube, fitted with the new mirrors, provided us with a device that could be switched on and off like an electric light bulb, required very little servicing, and took up much less space. Operating at one sixteenth of the power of the big tube, the micro-source delivered twenty-five percent of the former's intensity at the specimen. We improved the mirrors and more than doubled the intensity but, shortly afterwards, better mirrors were produced for the big X-ray tube, which now made it four times more intense than our set-up. As we made further improvements, so did the manufacturers of the big tubes. Although we finished with about ten times more intensity than in our first installation, we always remained slightly behind the monsters.

By this time, the contest had become somewhat meaningless: at synchrotron radiation sources, the X-ray intensity was another hundred to five hundred times higher and the making of X-ray measurements could be speeded up by this factor. What finally influenced my LMB colleagues almost to abandon using home-based X-ray sources and instead to travel to the European Synchrotron Research Facility (ESRF), in Grenoble, was that the funding for these journeys came from a European Union budget, instead of their own research grants. At the time of writing this (2005), strenuous efforts are being made to render unnecessary the presence of the investigator at the experiment. Instead, the apparatus could be controlled by data links from the computer console in the home laboratory of the crystallographers.

Not only has the X-ray examination of crystals been auto-mated and enormously accelerated: the production of the crystals, their crystallisation from solution, can now be carried out by robot machinery. Success in growing crystals depends on getting the temperature and the concentration of the solution and its acidity exactly right. The robots operate by filling a large number of crystallisation vessels automatically, each with a slightly different amount of additive, so that a large number of operations can be carried out simultaneously in order to determine the optimum conditions.

Hardware and software developments have made it possible for X-ray structure determinations to be carried out by people coming from other disciplines, such as organic chemistry, genetics or biochemistry, after a relatively short training. Some purists have expressed their concern that the principal investi-gators are being placed at too great a distance from the specimens that they are investigating; without a detailed knowledge of every step in the experiment, errors and false interpretations of the results can arise too easily. I think that these fears will remain baseless as long as good young people come into the field and decide how much they do not need to learn.

During my research career, I acquired a lot of skills that are no longer required today. Before one could use electronic techniques, one needed to know how to build the electronic circuitry, mostly from scratch. One started by bending up a sheet metal chassis and punching the necessary holes in it for mounting the components. The connecting wires had to be soldered without making dry joints. Somewhat later, one learnt to make printed circuit boards and to gold-plate the terminals in a cyanide bath. (There were no safety officers then.) One carried in one's head a lot of information, such as the pin layout of a number of commonly-used radio valves (vacuum tubes) and, later, one needed to know the characteristics of popular transistors. Physicists working with vacuum equipment, as most of them did, had their own recipes for vacuum greases; physical chemists had to be skilled glass blowers – in soda glass, which cracked unless it was annealed very, very slowly.

I do not think that research workers were more efficient or more productive in the old days, although arguably they had more fun. There was more satisfaction from work that was carried out with one or two colleagues; today one not uncommonly sees publications in which the list of collaborators or co-authors occupies more space than the abstract of the paper. Larger teams require a larger administrative staff, more time spent on writing grant applications, and more worries about one's paper's performance in the citation index (the assessment of a publication by how often it is referred to in other authors' papers).

Sandy Mathieson, with whom I have exchanged letters over many years, once wrote to me that he believed that soon the real research would be carried out only by the old, who were no longer under pressure to rush into publication and thus have time to brood and think. They know that the real satisfaction lies in solving or resolving problems and that it is not critical whether their work pays off in relation to others. Fortunately, there are still some younger scientists who are of the same mind and, even more fortunately, some of them can still discover important problems that do not require large teams and vast budgets.

In addition to my professional activities, we lived a busy and active life. We were lucky in that, since 1994, our three daughters and their families have all lived in England. Elizabeth and her husband, Roger Lilley, returned from a two-and-a-half-year round the world trip in 1991 and settled in Cambridge, Helen being born just after their return in 1991 and Edward in 1993. Caroline and Dick (Welch) came back to Hampshire in 1994 after more than four years in Florida with Jonathan, who was born in 1992. I had been able to combine visits to them with several business journeys and greatly enjoyed being shown the bird life and the alligators and turtles in the Everglades. I also had a brief introduction to snorkelling in the Florida Keys; unfortunately, my increasing asthma made breathing in a mask difficult for me. Imogen was born in 1995 and Katharine in 1997. Annabel married Nick Culver in 2003, their daughter, Poppy, was born in the same year, and Joseph in 2005.

Our own birthdays seemed to come round more and more quickly and our daughters saw to it that they were celebrated suitably. For my seventieth birthday, Annabel booked me a gliding lesson at nearby Duxford airfield. I enjoyed it greatly until I rashly asked the instructor behind me whether these gliders ever got into a spin and he proceeded to show me that they did. My eightieth birthday was celebrated by a hot air balloon flight in a party that included Roger and Edward. To keep the aerial tradition going, the three girls organised a seventieth birthday party for Valerie on the London Eye.

We did not travel as much or as far as our friends in their later years, but we did not do too badly. In 1987, we visited Crete. We arranged our programme ourselves and stayed in hotels recommended to us by our much-travelled daughters. We found ourselves on the same plane to Heraklion as some Cambridge acquaintances. On arrival, they were being organised by their tour leader as we engaged a taxi to take us to our hotel; they got back to England a week before us and reported that we had probably been abducted, as we had last been seen driven away by a villainous-looking driver. I do not know whether we were impressed more by the magnificent Cretan antiquities, the marvellous spring flowers or the friendliness of the Cretans.

We had two more walking holidays in Buttermere, the last one in 1996, when I had to admit regretfully that mountain-walking was no longer for me. The next year, we tried the Channel Islands and discovered Sark where, in the next four years, we spent very peaceful and quiet holidays. On each occasion, we flew to Guernsey and then crossed to Sark on a small ferry. This gave me the opportunity of seeing the dozens of rocks which stud the Little Russell Channel between the two islands, where I had sailed several times in my bachelor days. On looking at the hazards from a higher vantage point than the cockpit of a sailing boat, I was astonished that we had never hit anything while sailing. Once, we had even entered St Peter Port, Guernsey, in the dark. In those days, one anchored in the outer basin, which was always over-crowded in summer, so that one had to be prepared to fend off one's neighbours when all boats were swinging at the change of the tide.

Today, St Peter Port has two large marinas, where hundreds of boats are moored in dredged basins fitted with locks, so that they do not dry out at low tide. The range of spring tides is more than twenty feet. The tale was told before the marinas were built of strangers coming ashore from an anchored yacht at high water and tying up their dinghy with a short painter. When they came back at low water, the dinghy was hanging vertically six feet above the water. They learnt their lesson: the next time, they came ashore at low water and, this time, tied their long painter to a rung of the ladder leading to the top of the jetty. When they returned from their shore excursion the dinghy was afloat, but the knot was fifteen feet below the surface of the water. We had no such problems during our holidays on Sark, where we navigated on hired bicycles.

We did, however, do some sailing several times in the Solent and along the south coast as far as Weymouth with Caroline and Dick, Jonathan, Imogen, and Katharine. At first they chartered, and then for a number of years they owned, a cruising catamaran. We both had pretty good cast iron stomachs, so Valerie did valiant duty in the saloon as a floating baby sitter when the weather was rough, while I enjoyed taking the wheel. I was much impressed by the convenience of a modern boat compared with those I was sailing when I was young. Manoeuvring under power in a crowded harbour (they are all crowded these days), one could spin the catamaran right round with one engine going forward and the other in reverse. I had never before been shipmates with such elaborate electronic equipment, which included an autopilot that maintained a steadier course than I could keep to manually. The global positioning indicator fed its computer, which could work out the speed over the ground and display it on the console in front of the helmsman, together with the depth of water, as recorded by the echo sounder. I thought how wrong I had been in the 1950s when a colleague in the lab who was a specialist in ultrasonics asked me whether there would be a market for an echo sounder for yachts. I answered that such a device would never work because small boats could not provide a suitably dry environment for electronics. In my justification, I must say that this was before the invention of the transistor, when all electronics relied on vacuum tubes that needed high-voltage supplies.

I had another opportunity to admire modern nautical advances. In July 1999, we travelled on the Norwegian coastal service from Bergen to the North Cape and back. During this cruise, we went on a tour of the bridge, which looked like the computer console which, of course, it was. The two helmsmen, in short sleeves, sat in front of the computer displays. The global positioning indicator kept the ship's position within five metres of the pre-calculated course. Had there been any necessity of making a course alteration, it could be made with a joystick. Our cruise lived up to its boast of being the most beautiful journey in the world. The passage past the Lofoten Islands had a peculiarly magic quality. All the way there were magnificent views of the coast by day and at night under the midnight sun. A feature of the Norwegian coastal voyage is that the passengers are a mixture of foreign tourists, mainly German, English, Dutch, and French, and Norwegians for whom this is the normal way of travelling up and down the coast.

161

We had two very different holidays in Florence. On our first visit to that lovely city, we were by ourselves and concentrated on the well-known sights. In the restored house of a fourteenth century merchant, we tacked ourselves on to an Italian University of the Third Age group by kind permission of their lecturer whose Tuscan Italian was so clear that we understood most of what he said. In the interesting Museum of Science and Technology, behind the Uffici, I explained the exhibits of Toricelli's and Galileo's apparatus to Valerie and found that I had become the guide, being followed by a small group. One of the pleasing aspects of Italy is that entry to many museums is free for the over-sixty-fives from European Union countries. Is it xenophobic to feel that this pleasure is enhanced by the fact that the Americans and the Japanese have to pay?

Our second visit to Florence was with a group of Friends of the Fitzwilliam Museum, led by Duncan Robinson, the director of the museum, whose enthusiasm is always infectious, and who showed us a number of lesser-known churches and museums, which we would never have discovered for ourselves.

We went on a few other Friends' tours, among them a visit to the Vermeer exhibition in Holland in 1996. I found this exhibition very slightly disappointing, probably because I had seen nearly all the paintings many times in the Hague, London, Berlin, and New York, under much less crowded conditions. But, unexpectedly, we were more than compensated by an exhibition that we saw in the Prinsenshof in Delft, on our way home, of 'Vermeer's Contemporaries of the Golden Period'. This was a wonderful collection of pictures that had been temporarily displaced from the Mauritshuis by the main exhibition, together with many other paintings from other Dutch museums – and all in uncrowded galleries! I wonder whether single-artist collections or exhibitions are not basically for the expert specialist, rather than for people like me who know very little about art but know what they like.

We attended a Cambridge University extension course of lectures on Byzantine and early Christian Art and followed this with a package holiday to Ravenna, Cividale, Poros, and Venice. The calm and formal mosaics that we saw in Ravenna were an interesting contrast with the lively mosaics in the Naples Museum of Antiquities, which houses so many objects excavated in Pompeii and Herculaneum, that we saw on another cultural holiday the following year.

Our last and longest tour with the Friends of the Fitzwilliam Museum was in 2002 to St Petersburg. We spent two complete days in the Hermitage, visited the Peterhof and Zarske Selo (my father's place of birth, but I do not know where he lived there). One of the pleasant surprises was the very fine Russian painters of the Victorian period, who deserve to be known much better than they are. We also saw a rehearsal in the Mariinsky Ballet school, some magnificent dancing in the Hermitage Theatre, and a performance of *Boris Godunov*.

Books and reading

Books started to form an important part of my life at an early stage. One of my earliest memories is of my mother telling me that the next book she would read to me would be different: it would not have a number of separate stories but instead there would be one story starting at the beginning of the book and finishing at the end, and this story would be broken up into parts called chapters. I would have one chapter read out at bedtime and would have to go to sleep after that.

I do not remember many of my early childhood books, but one day, when I was in the United States in my thirties, I was taken by my hosts in Colorado to visit friends of theirs, German immigrants, who lived in pretty complete isolation in the forest. On the kitchen table was a children's book about three rabbits, printed in Gothic letters, which I immediately recognised as having had it read to me while I was in the kindergarten in Berlin.

When I was between four and six, I was given a new 'Doctor Dolittle' book by Hugh Lofting every year at Christmas and I remember the thrill when I discovered that I could read the third volume by myself and did not have to wait for an adult to read it to me. I no longer know what came between Doctor Dolittle and the Greek and Nordic Myths. I suppose it must have been the classic German children's stories by Hoffmann and by Wihelm Busch and others like them. When I came across these books many years later, I thought them much too cruel and sadistic for my own children. There was *Struwwelpeter*, 'Shock-headed Peter', who had his fingers cut off because he would not stop biting his nails (clearly illustrated with floods of blood dripping from the stumps), Max and Moritz, the mice who were ground up like corn by the miller, whom they had teased, and then eaten up by the chickens, and many more delightful and instructive tales.

For the somewhat older age group, there were German classics like Baron Münchhausen (an eighteenth century teller of tall tales) and the traditional stories of the wise fool, Till Eulenspiegel. In addition, German publishers went in on a large scale for 'translations' and adaptations of foreign classics. Everyone knew that the name 'Robinson Crusoe' must be a misprint because Robinson, surely, was a surname; so the castaway in the German edition was called Crusoe Robinsohn with an 'H'. Very considerable liberties were taken with Defoe's novel. The Swiss Family Robinsons' island, of course, was a zoological and botanical impossibility, serving as a platform for Victorian, or rather Wilhelmine, morality lessons.

The only modern children's fiction I can remember was the novels by Erich Kästner: *Emil and the Detectives* and *Lotte and Lisa* were both turned into successful films. The former was set and filmed in the part of Berlin where we lived and the latter was much later an Anglo-American production, with Hayley Mills in the title role. A favourite of mine was a translation from the Swedish of Selma Lagerlöf's *Wonderful Journey of Nils Holgersson*, which was appreciated just as much by my daughters when we read it as a bedtime book.

I have more vivid memories of the serial stories that appeared in my weekly boys' magazine. At least one of them seems to have been written like a modern TV 'soap' to follow current events in a politically correct way. It started with the hero in the German Scouts (*Wandervögel*); after Hitler came to power in 1933, the entire patrol changed uniforms and joined the Hitler Youth.

Among the then-modern German science fiction writers was Hans Dominik, whose German heroes always behaved in a saint-like manner in the face of sinister Japanese, cheating Americans, sporting but ineffectual Italians, and incompetent British and French. One of his novels was about an international round-the-world air race in which the Germans possess a futuristic aeroplane (jet?), capable of flying at a thousand kilometres an hour, but which they are too fair to set in direct competition against the less reliable conventional American (500 km/h) and British (450 km/h) planes. They prefer to win the race with a superbly well-functioning 420 km/h plane, only to amaze the world by beating the next competitor into third place by flying their jet halfway round the world to get to the finishing line in time.

I read many German historical novels, which were popular and in plentiful supply. The principal characters in them were usually young German boys who fought valiantly by the side of Armenius against the invading Roman legions of Varro, Teutonic maidens who were rescued from the jaws of savage animals in Nero's circuses by Germanic Christian slaves, Ostrogoths and other honorary Germans, who were victorious for a while against Romans and Byzantines, and heroic youths who single-handedly routed Attila the Hun. (The Huns at that time were non-aryan according to Nazi ideology.) There were German orphans who suffered bullying, by inferior foreigners, in the Thirty Years War, boys who became drummers in the heroic army of Frederick the Great or freedom fighters against Napoleon's armies. There were the soldiers who were victorious in World War I but who, unfortunately, were stabbed in the back by Jews and Communists.

It all taught me some history, even if it was from a highly distorted viewpoint, which my parents tried to correct as far as possible. My enthusiasm for armies and battles tied in with my collection of thirty millimetre-high tin soldiers, many of them hand painted in the correct uniforms of their period. I still have Roman legionnaires and Carthaginian cavalry, colourful Turkish troops as they appeared before Vienna, Prussian infantry and cavalry and their Austrian adversaries in the Seven Years' War, and many hundreds of soldiers of the Napoleonic era. My interest in the colourful uniforms of the past has left me with the ability to date the uniforms in paintings, or in museum displays, with an accuracy of better than thirty years over a considerable period of European history.

The bias in some of the international classics of historical fiction, such as Bulwer Lytton's *Last Days of Pompeii*, Henryk Sienkiewicz's *Quo Vadis* and Lew Wallace's *Ben Hur*, was somewhat different. In all of these, Christianity triumphs over paganism. The partisan support of German writers like Felix Dahn and Gustav Freytag, in contrast, evoked the readers' sympathies for the heroic Teutonic pagans in their opposition to the pale and effete Christians. Edited and retold versions of the Nordic Legends and Sagas were also very popular. The Nordic gods were made to be more interesting and full-blooded than the Greeks and Romans: there was more fighting and more manly drinking and one was less exposed to soppy tales like those about Penelope and other virtuous women.

I have few recollections of German boys' or, for that matter girls', stories for the teenagers of the interwar period, possibly because when I had reached the age for them I had left Germany and was mainly reading English books. I suppose books written for that readership were pretty violently jingoist and xenophobic in all countries. I can only think of Dornford Yates' thugs who were allowed to practise acts of mayhem against the wrong sort of foreigners (Germans and Jews), as long as they retained their gentleman-like behaviour towards the right sort of foreigners (Austrian peasants, Ruritanian aristocrats and beautiful French girls). And Jules Verne's Englishmen were not exactly calculated to promote enthusiasm for the Entente Cordiale among French readers.

When I came to England at the age of twelve it was a little while before I started to appreciate English humorous authors, whether Lewis Carroll, Richmal Crompton, Stella Gibbon or PG Wodehouse. In the film *Pimpernel Smith*, Sydney Greenstreet is a fat SS officer who reads *Jabberwock* to Leslie Howard, interrupting himself every few lines with 'dat iss not fonny, eh?' At one time, I would have sympathised: I remember being completely at a loss to understand the paroxisms of laughter from a friend who was reading *Just William* while he was staying with us.

At first, the required reading at school took up most of my energy: I found Scott (*Ivanhoe* and *The Talisman*) quite a struggle and understanding Shakespeare was even more of a problem. The only plays I ever read in school were *Midsummer Night's Dream* and *The Tempest*, surely both of them much less appealing to boys in their early teens than the histories!

The Greek and Latin set books provided quite a stimulus to my reading. It did not need much discernment to realise that the excerpts from Xenophon's *Anabasis* and from Herodotus were rattling good tales and that it was worthwhile reading more than selected snippets, of course, in English translations. Having 'done' Book Two of the *Aeneid* and parts of a book of Thucydides'

History I wanted to read the other books, again in translation. I never got as far as Homer in Greek lessons at school, but I had greatly enjoyed *The Iliad* and *The Odyssey* when I was about ten. My granddaughter Helen read the Rieu translation of *The Odyssey* when she was seven. I was sorry that I could not provide an answer when she had finished it and wanted to know what she should read next that was as good!

Some enthusiasms were counter-productive. My form master cackled with delight when he read some of Macauley's essays to us and rammed them down our throats to such an extent that I swore to myself that I would never have anything more to do with any of Macauley's writings. About forty years later I happened to pick up his *History of England* and was completely hooked. At a time when it had become fashionable to take a gloomy view of the past, and of the future, it is a real pleasure to absorb the Whig view, with its firm belief in its own correctness and its faith in a continuing progress towards a better and better world.

My reading became wider once School Certificate was out of the way. I was given a subscription to Boots Book-lovers' Library and always kept a full list of books that I wanted to read at the local branch, eagerly consulting the book reviews in *The Observer* every week. I suspect that the fact that most librarians tended to be rather attractive young women contributed to the frequency of my library visits. I have always regretted that I have lost the lists I made of the books I read as a schoolboy and later, but I know that I discovered modern fiction writers like JB Priestley, AJ Cronin, James Hilton, Hugh Walpole, and John Galsworthy.

None of the books on modern science that I read as a boy seemed to have made a lasting impression on me. I was probably put off Eddington's *Mysterious Universe* by Susan Stebbing's *Philosophy and the Physicists*, and her condemnation of the excursions into philosophy by various writers on physics. I have the impression that German and, to a slightly lesser extent, French scientists were very much more concerned with the philosophical implications of quantum mechanics and relativity theory than were British and American scientists. The great German theoretical physicist, Werner Heisenberg, in his writings, comes back several times to the revolutionary concepts that had been introduced by the modern theories, and says that any scientist who is not worried by quantum mechanics does not understand what it is all about.

What I read profitably after school certificate was Sherwood Taylor's *World of Science*, a sort of all-you-need-to–know-about-all-branches-of-science. I still have my copy and find it an interesting insight into what one did not need to know in 1938.

On the whole, I have been less interested in the biographies of great scientists of the past than in the lives of statesman and politicians. Perhaps the scientists' beards were too large and their collars too high and stiff, but probably their biographies discuss only their interactions with other scientists and, to make sense of these, one has to understand too much of the details of controversies that are now less relevant.

I never derived much pleasure from detective stories. It has always struck me as a little nasty to get one's enjoyment from detailed accounts of murders. During most of my life, I have been occupied in solving puzzles set by nature and so I am not greatly attracted to solving invented mysteries. (I use the same arguments for avoiding being drawn into playing chess or bridge.) For light relief, I have always preferred science fiction to crime stories. Unlike my friend and former colleague, David Blow, who, in the last year of his life, wrote a clever and original science fiction novel, I have not succeeded in producing such a tale myself.

Before 1939, the sources of books for middle-class readers were rather different from today. They borrowed their books from one of the private subscription libraries like Boots, W H Smith, or *The Times* library; public municipal lending libraries were somewhat outside the sphere (was it a fear of infection?). Alternatively, one bought cheap edition hardbacks. The mass sales of paperbacks really only got going in the last year or two before the war. For commuters and travellers, reading matter of a reasonable quality was available from a large number of weeklies and monthlies, such as the *Strand Magazine, Punch, Lilliput,* and many others. It was in the *Strand Magazine* that I first came across Agatha Christie's Hercule Poirot short stories.

Probably because I did not come from a conventional British family background, I did not start on the English classics, Jane

Austen, Dickens, Trollope, Thackeray, and the Brontës until much later in life. Instead, I devoured the Russians during my last year at school. I have a feeling that this was the correct age to read Dostoyevsky. When I came back to Russian novels in my thirties and forties, I found the psychology of the characters very difficult to empathise with. At that time I had just discovered Tolkien's *Lord of the Rings* and I found his hobbits, elves, and dwarves more understandable than the Karamazovs.

When I went up to Cambridge I was, of course, educated by my peers, not only in the classics and in political and travel books, but also in the common heritage of children's books. I could not go on totally ignorant of Eyore, Kanga, and Roo and completely failing to understand any reference to Mr Toad. And mathematical physics and quantum mechanics are crying out for quotations from *Alice Through the Looking-Glass*.

As a research student, I had a little more time for relaxation reading than I had had as an undergraduate and I made much use of the large second-hand book department in Heffers' old Petty Cury premises. The staff there seemed able to lay their hands on any requested paperbacks on two floors and to quote appropriate prices (ordinary fiction and detective stories six pence, soft pornography nine pence or a shilling). Then, as now, I have loved using the university library, although I have always been a little afraid of the librarians. They do not actually answer an inquiry for a book with the words, 'You only want it because you think it is pornographic, you would not understand it, but in any case we have not got it' but that is the answer one can see on their faces. I like the old catalogue in the huge volumes, into which generations of librarians' widows have carefully pasted the individual entries, much better than I like the computer catalogue, which seems to work in a different way each time I use the library.

Shortly after this new catalogue came in, I wanted to settle an argument with my son-in-law, Roger, about something in the Gospel of St. John. I typed in 'St. John' and got the response 'St Kilda, bird life on'. So I entered, 'Gospel', only to receive 'Gosport, Hants, population statistics'. I found a librarian who rather scornfully repeated what I had done with the same results and then told me that I should have typed 'Bible', of course, which he did so quickly that he left out the second 'b' in 'Bible', and so the answer came back 'Bile duct, diseases of'. When he found me the microfiche from the old catalogue, there was an entire fiche on the Gospel of St. John. I cannot remember what the argument had been about, but Roger had been right.

I tried to chase up books in second-hand bookshops wherever I went. On one occasion, in a shop in Hay-on-Wye, it was the other way round and a book pursued and caught me. I had been looking through historical books when a fat volume fell into my lap from an upper shelf. It proved to be a biography, in English, of Ernst Moritz Arndt, a nationalist German writer and politician (1769–1860), who might have been a remote relative of mine. Of course, I bought the book, which had an interesting account of Arndt's life during the Napoleonic wars, when he fled through a series of European countries (always just ahead of the French armies), finally to return in the wake of the Russian armies after Napoleon's retreat from Moscow. It was a very different world from that of *A Tale of Two Cities* or of *The Scarlet Pimpernel*, where there was always a safe English haven in the background.

The next chapter in the history of my involvement with books started when I first bought books to read to our children. I remember being shown something in Hatchards' children's department that I thought too difficult for a five and a three-year-old.

'I assure you, sir,' said the shop assistant, 'this book uses only four letter words.'

'In that case I consider it highly unsuitable for my daughters,' I replied. This would not have happened in Heffers in Cambridge, where we soon got all our books. The children's department there was presided over for many years by Miss Tinling, whose advice was always excellent and as though she knew all her customers' children personally.

For many years, almost until Annabel left school, we had a session of reading aloud every evening at bedtime for about twenty minutes. The lion's share of the reading fell to me so that Valerie could get on with some sewing during the session. The choice of books was very catholic. I think we started with Pooh and Paddington Bear (but never Beatrix Potter, whom for some reason I could not stand), went on to *Doctor Dolittle* and *Children of the New Forest*, to *Nils Holgerson* and to *Swallows and Amazons*. (It was quite some years later that I discovered that Roger Walker of the *Swallows* was based on Roger Altounyan, almost a contemporary of mine at Emmanuel College, who became a distinguished physician).

We also read non-fiction: Thor Heyerdahl's *Kontiki* went down better than John Hunt's *Ascent of Everest*. Cherry Gerard's *Worst Journey* was the most appreciated of this genre. Then there were the Narnia books by CS Lewis (I was surprised to discover some years later that the analogy with Christianity had escaped Annabel at the time), and the adult science fiction by the same author. We read Homer relatively early, greatly enjoyed *The Lord of the Rings*, struggled through some Walter Scott, were thrilled by *The Riddle of the Sands*, by *The Thirty-Nine Steps* and a few others of John Buchan's adventure books. We enjoyed Baroness Orczy's *The Scarlet Pimpernel*, but thought all her later sequels mere potboilers. Not surprisingly, Dickens read aloud very well, especially *A Tale of Two Cities* and *A Christmas Carol*. We all cried over *The Prisoner of Zenda*, laughed at *Cold Comfort Farm* and enjoyed Churchill's *My Early Life*. There were no strict selection rules other than that the books had to be of interest to all of us and, usually, that they were not what the girls would have read on their own.

I think our sessions bound us together as a family. It was always a hollow threat, 'if you do not do such and such, there will be no reading tonight', because the girls knew that we enjoyed it as much as they did. Our grandchildren have also enjoyed having books read to them and Helen now reads to a blind neighbour once a week. *The Swiss Family Robinson* and *The Pickwick Papers* have been on her list.

I have said above that I am sorry that I have never been sufficiently organised to persevere with keeping a list of books that I have read. But since 1977 I have kept a commonplace book in which I have jotted down memorable quotations from books which I have read, odd or surprising facts, and unexpected statistics. I have been inspired by John Julius Norwich, who has published a number of 'Christmas Crackers', being selections from the current year's commonplace book. I have found it an enjoyable and inexpensive hobby. Lord Norwich's rule is not to hunt for the nuggets, but only to set down what has come his way accidentally. I do not agree: I want some sort of a written record of how virtuous I have been in reading the whole of Gibbon's *Decline and Fall* from cover to cover, from which I have written down many quotations. But since practically every sentence is quote-worthy, I do not need to apologise for my practice. Equally, it was probably sheer swank to write down quite a few quotations in their original Latin, French or German, and to have one Russian quotation. But to atone for my boasting, here is what Congreve said in *The Way of the World*:

> Thou art a retailer of phrases
> And dost deal in remnants of remnants
> Like a maker of pincushions.

And this is Montesquieu in *Lettres Persanes LXVII*:

> Of all authors, there are none whom I dislike more than the compilers who look everywhere for scraps from the work of others, which they insert in their own writing like turves in a garden bed. They are in no way superior to the workers in a print shop who arrange the letters that will, when combined together, be turned into a book, towards which they have contributed only manual labour. I want respect to be shown to the original books and it seems to me to be a kind of desecration to pull the component pieces from their sanctuary and to expose them to a disapproval that they do not merit.

Alone, 2004–2005

The year 2004 started well enough. Valerie had been receiving radiotherapy and chemotherapy treatment for some years for breast cancer and, early in the year, she was declared to be in remission and no further treatment was needed.

In March 2004, Valerie came back uncharacteristically tired from a nine-mile ramble, but she rallied sufficiently to organise festivities to celebrate my eightieth birthday in April. The five older grandchildren are all musical and formed a fine orchestra. Tony and Eve Fisher came over from Kent and Victoria Viebahn (née Hackforth-Jones) with her husband Christoph flew in from Germany.

Shortly afterwards, Valerie started to suffer from breathlessness and anaemia. She was diagnosed as having myeloma and went into hospital for a month; she rallied somewhat after blood transfusions. The summer and autumn were relatively normal and Valerie was able to enjoy having friends visiting her in the garden and even to go to the theatre. However, in November her anaemia became much worse and she was again admitted into hospital where she spent four very uncomfortable weeks and died three days before Christmas. I shall never cease missing her, but it is a consolation to know that she did not have a long period of failing powers, which she would have hated.

She had continued her very active life until her final confinement in hospital. She had even gone to her clinic sessions by bicycle. She ran her play-reading group for the University of the Third Age with great enthusiasm and her loyal class followed her from year to year. As a Friend of the Fitzwilliam Museum, she took her turn at the information desk, she sang with a local choral group, was the main prop of a French circle, was on the committee of the Cambridge Jane Austen Society, where she contributed several much-appreciated talks, and she walked regularly with the Rambling Club. She had been instrumental in persuading neighbours in Barrow Road to replant the avenue of cherry trees when old ones died or became diseased. As the 'tree-lady', as a neighbourhood watch convener, as a distributor of the parish magazine, and as an organiser of street parties from time to time, she greatly helped to make Barrow Road into an exceptionally friendly neighbourhood.

On top of her outside activities, she was a constant support to her daughters in all problems and vicissitudes and she was a loving and much-loved grandmother to her grandchildren. Valerie's keen mind and wide knowledge were always available to answer any questions put to her by the family: her daughters called her 'mummy dot info'; when they were small, they believed that Valerie had been the sole author of the *Oxford English Dictionary* as well as of the *Petit Larousse*. Her intelligence was applied to every aspect of daily life, whether it was the most economical way of cutting out her dress material or the most efficient way of parking a car in a tight spot. Valerie had, to an exceptional extent, the ability to see links and connections between apparently unrelated facts or events. It was this that made her such an interesting conversationalist and such an inspiring teacher to her students, as well as to her husband and daughters and her grandchildren.

Valerie was very modest about her academic 'failures'. She had not got into Oxbridge and did not get a particularly good degree at London University. To me, these failures always seemed good examples of what was wrong with English girls' schools and women's colleges fifty years ago. Valerie's logical brain would have made her an excellent mathematician, but mathematics was not taught in the sixth form of her school. When she read French and Spanish at Westfield College, it should have been obvious that her interests were in linguistics rather than in the study of romantic literature.

Among Valerie's outstanding qualities were her complete integrity and honesty. She was incapable of dissimulation or of telling a white lie. In her school and student days, she was often picked for a part in a play in view of her beautiful speaking voice but it always became obvious that Valerie was no actress; she found it impossible to play a part or to pretend to be anyone other than herself.

She had inherited her quick and intelligent mind from her parents. She was fond of telling how her father had once presented her with an open copy of *The Times* and asked her which news item in that day's paper she considered least likely to be true. Politically, Valerie was a life-long liberal, with both a small and a capital 'L'. She was a convinced European from a natural inclination and as a result of close friendships with French and other European acquaintances. She was a devoted, but not aggressive, Anglican. It was a sorrow to her that her doctrinal differences with the vicar and her conscience drove her from Trumpington Church, where she had worshipped under previous incumbents and where she had been a member of the parochial church council.

Life with Valerie was always fun. She had an uncanny ability to meet interesting people and to draw them out. I remember conversations with a French judge in a restaurant on the Ile d'Yeu, with a choral scholar on the King's Cross to Cambridge train, and with a Hebrew scholar who was doing a right-to-left crossword puzzle on a train. For forty-six years, I came home every evening wondering what interesting things Valerie was going to tell me and on which of the day's events I should want her views and opinions.

More than a hundred people came to Valerie's memorial service, for which she herself had chosen the hymns. Helen and Edward played a movement of JS Bach's *Concerto for Two Violins*, accompanied by Roger. The second lesson was read by Jonathan, and Dick read my tribute to Valerie, with additions from our three daughters.

Postscript

Uli died at home on 24 March 2006 of malignant melanoma. To the relief of his family, he suffered little pain and retained his clear mind until the end. We are immensely grateful for the kindness shown by his many friends, neighbours and carers in his last months.

Writing this autobiography meant a huge amount to Uli. He started work on it immediately after the death of our mother Valerie. He wanted the book to be as much a tribute to their marriage as a record of his career and its writing occupied much of the time which he would so much rather have spent talking to Valerie. Despite a life-long indifference to the use of computers for recreational purposes, he taught himself how to use the necessary dictation software. He would often work far into the night, making himself hoarse and leaving his supper to get cold.

Although sadly Uli did not live to see publication of the book, he had the satisfaction of seeing the cover and page proofs while at home in his final weeks. He was modestly surprised at the interest family and friends had shown in his writing and had started to plan a second book of memoirs.

People came from as far afield as California to attend his memorial service. This was a moving tribute to our wonderful and talented father.

Elizabeth Arndt
Caroline Welch
Annabel Culver

Printed in the United Kingdom
by Lightning Source UK Ltd.
116565UKS00001B/4-33